EXPLORING SCIENCE

TRAINS

RAILWAYS • TUNNELS • SIGNALS • DIESEL • STEAM

With 10 easy-to-do experiments and 230 exciting pictures

MICHAEL HARRIS AND STEVE PARKER

ARMADILLO

This edition is published by Armadillo, an imprint of Anness Publishing Ltd
www.armadillobooks.co.uk; www.annesspublishing.com; Twitter: @Anness_Books

Anness Publishing has a picture agency outlet for images for publishing,
promotions or advertising. Please visit our website www.practicalpictures.com
for more information.

Publisher: Joanna Lorenz
Principal Text Contributor: Jackie Gaff
Project Editors: Jenni Davidson, Leon Gray and Elizabeth Young
Designer: Caroline Reeves, Aztec Design
Special Photography: John Freeman
Stylist: Melanie Williams
Picture Researcher: Gwen Campbell
Illustrator: Peter Bull Art Studio
Production Controller: Pirong Wang

We would like to thank the following children, and their parents, for appearing in this
book: Tyrone Agiton, Erin Bhogal, Stacie Damps, Brooke Griffiths, Eddie Lengthorn,
Nicky Payne, Zoe Richardson and Ajvir Sandhu.

PICTURE CREDITS
b=bottom, t=top, c=central, l=left, r=right
Alvey and Towers Picture Library: 22cl, 31tl, 41t, 41cl, 41br, 49c, 57br; Anthony J. Lambert
Collection: 4t, 21tr, 23br, 48tl, 55tl; Colin Boocock: 25br; Corbis/Morton Beebe, S.F.: 57t;
Corbis/Bettmann: 27cl; Corbis/Dallas and John Heaton: 56b; Corbis/John Heseltine: 23bl;
Corbis/Jeremy Horner: 34tl; Corbis/Hulton Getty: 40cl; Corbis/Wolfgang Kaehler: 49b;
Corbis/Lake County Museum: 5t; Corbis/Milepost 92½: 37tl;
Corbis/Paul A. Souders: 25tl; Corbis/Michael S. Yamashita: 27tr,
32b, 46tr; Danjaq/Eon Productions/The Kobal Collection: 53tr;
Chris Dixon: 1; Richard Griffin/www.squarewheels.org.uk:
33cl; Mike Harris: 2t, 57cr; HTT/JumpStartFund/Omegabyte:
59bl; The Illustrated London News: 38t, 38br, 48bl; The Kobal
Collection: 52bl, 52br, 53tl, 53bl, 53br, 63bl; London
Underground Ltd: 15cr; Mary Evans Picture Library: 12b, 14t,
15t, 15cl, 16t, 16b, 20t, 20c, 22tl, 26tr, 26b, 36cr, 36bl, 40br;
Milepost 92½: 2b, 3cl, 3bl, 4c, 5cl, 6t, 8b, 9bl, 9br, 10t, 13cl, 13cr, 17c, 17b, 18t, 20b, 21tl,
21cr, 21b, 22cr, 23t, 24t, 24b, 25tr, 25bl, 27b, 31tr, 33cr, 37cl, 37br, 39tl, 39cl, 42tr, 44bl,
44br, 45c, 45b, 48br, 50tr, 52tr, 58t, 59cr, 62tr; Millbrook House Ltd: 26c, 28tl; Brian
Morrison: 13b, 63tr; Network Rail Media Centre: 5cr, 33t, 45t; QA Photos Ltd: 39cr;
Claire Rae: 55cr; RAWIE: 33bl, 33bc; Science and Society/National Railway Museum: 3tr,
3cr, 8t, 36t, 54b, 60t; Science and Society/London Transport Museum: 40tl; SNCF-
CAV/Sylvain Cambon: 15b; SNCF-CAV/Jean-Marc Fabbro: 30b; Wikimedia
Commons/Helmut W. Hoffmann: 57cl; Wikimedia Commons/Frank Murmann
58br; Wikimedia Commons/Jackson Myers 58bl; Wikimedia
Commons/Picasa 59tl.

PUBLISHER'S NOTE

Manufacturer: Anness Publishing Ltd, 108 Great Russell Street,
London WC1B 3NA, England
For Product Tracking go to: www.annesspublishing.com/tracking
Batch: 7340-23380-1127

CONTENTS

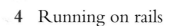

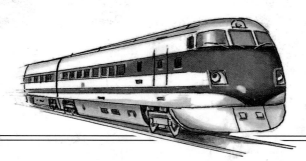

RUNNING ON RAILS

THROUGHOUT HISTORY, people have looked for ways to move themselves and their possessions faster and more efficiently. Wheels were invented well over 5,500 years ago. As wheels are round, they turn well on smooth surfaces and reduce the rubbing, slowing force called friction. However, it soon became clear that wheels do not work well on rough, soft or muddy ground.

To solve this problem, tracks of wood or stone were cut into or laid on to the ground to provide a smooth surface on which wheels could turn. This kept friction to a minimum, so that vehicles could move more easily and shift heavier loads.

The ancient Greeks made the first railed tracks around 400BC by cutting grooved rails into rock. They hauled ships overland by setting them on wheeled trolleys that ran along the tracks. Iron rails came into use in Europe by the mid-1700s. They were laid, mainly within mines, to transport coal or metal ores. Steam-powered locomotives were developed in the early 1800s. Before then, wagons in mines were pulled by horses or by the miners themselves, which was slow and only possible for short distances.

Pulling power
A horse pulls a freight wagon along rails. Modern railways developed from ones first laid in European mines in the mid-1500s. Heavy loads, such as coal and metal ore, were carried in wagons with wheels that ran along wooden planks. The wagons were guided by a peg underneath, which slotted into a gap between the planks. Horses and sometimes even human labourers were used to haul the wagons long before steam locomotives were invented.

Riding rails
It is just possible to make out the grooves where iron rails were laid at the Penydarran Ironworks in South Wales in the early 1800s. The world's first steam-powered train ran along these rails on 13 February 1804. The locomotive was designed by British engineer Richard Trevithick and hauled wagons 14.5km/9 miles at a speed of 8kmh/5mph.

1769–1810	1811–1830	1831–1860	1861–1880
1769 FRENCHMAN NICHOLAS CUGNOT builds the first steam-powered vehicle.	**1825** THE STOCKTON AND DARLINGTON Railway opens in Britain – the first public railway to use steam-powered locomotives.	**1833** GEORGE STEPHENSON devises the steam brake cylinder to operate brake blocks on the driving wheels of steam locomotives.	**1863** LONDON UNDERGROUND'S Metropolitan Line opens and is the world's first underground passenger railway.
	1827 THE BALTIMORE AND OHIO Railroad is chartered to run from Baltimore to the River Ohio, Virginia, in the USA.		**1864** AMERICAN GEORGE PULLMAN builds the first sleeping car, the *Pioneer*.
1804 BRITISH ENGINEER RICHARD TREVITHICK tests the first steam locomotive for the Penydarran Ironworks in Wales.			**1868** PULLMAN BUILDS the first dining car.
	1829 ROBERT AND GEORGE STEPHENSON'S *Rocket* wins the Rainhill Trials. It becomes the locomotive used for the Liverpool and Manchester Railway.		**1869** THE CENTRAL PACIFIC and Union Pacific railroads meet at Promontory Summit, linking the east and west coasts of America.
1808 TREVITHICK BUILDS a circular railway in London, Britain, and exhibits the *Catch Me Who Can* locomotive.		**1840s** SEMAPHORE SIGNALS are introduced. First tickets for train journeys are issued.	**1872** AMERICAN GEORGE WESTINGHOUSE patents an automatic air-braking system.

Trackless trains

Trackless trains run at many large museums, exhibitions and theme parks. They carry passengers in carts or wagons running rubber-tyred wheels on a road-like surface. Trains are pulled by an integral-combustion or electric unit made to look like a railway locomotive – or almost anything else.

Puffing Billy

The locomotive in this painting was nicknamed *Puffing Billy* because it was one of the earliest to have a chimney. It was designed by British mine engineer William Hedley and built in 1813. The first steam engines were built in the early 1700s. They were used to pump water from mineshafts, not to power vehicles. *Puffing Billy* can be seen today in the Science Museum in London, England. It is the world's oldest surviving steam locomotive.

Modern rail networks

Today, nearly all countries in the world have their own rail network. Thousands of kilometres of track criss-cross the continents. Steam power has now given way to newer inventions. Most modern trains are hauled by locomotives powered by diesel engines, by electricity drawn from overhead cables or from an electrified third rail on the track.

1881–1900	1901–1950	1951–1980	1981–present
1883 The luxurious *Orient Express* first runs on 5 June from Paris, France, to Bucharest in Romania.	**1901** The first commercial monorail opens in Wuppertal, northwestern Germany.	**1955** The world's most powerful single-unit diesel-electric locomotives, the Deltics, first run between London and Liverpool.	**1981** TGV (*Train à Grande Vitesse*) first runs between Paris and Lyon in France.
1893 The New York Central and Hudson River Railroad claims that its steam locomotive *No. 999* travels faster than 100mph (160kmh).	**1904** The New York City subway opens.	**1957** Trans-Europ Express (TEE) fleet of trains operates an international rail service across western Europe.	
	1938 *Mallard* sets the speed record for a steam locomotive (203kmh/126mph).	**1964** The Bullet Train first runs on the *Tōkaidō Shinkansen* between Tokyo and Osaka in Japan.	**1994** Channel Tunnel completed, linking rail networks in Britain and the Continent.
1895 Baltimore and Ohio No. 1 is the first electric locomotive to run on the mainline Baltimore and Ohio Railroad.	**1940s** Union Pacific Big Boys are built by the American Locomotive Company.	**1980** The first maglev (magnetic levitation) service opens at Birmingham Airport.	**2004** Shanghai Maglev Train, the first commercial maglev system, opens in China.
1900 Paris *Métro* opens.			

RAILWAY TRACK

A FULLY LADEN train is heavy, so the track it runs on has to be tough. Nowadays, rails are made from steel, which is a much stronger material than the cast iron used for the first railways. The shape of the rail also helps to make it tough. If you sliced through a rail from top to bottom you would see it has an 'I'-shaped cross section. The broad, flat bottom narrows into the 'waist' of the I and widens again into a curved head. Most countries use a rail shaped like this.

Tracks are lengths of rail, which are laid on wooden or concrete crossbeams called sleepers, or ties. Train wheels are a set distance apart, so rails must be the same. The distance between rails is called the gauge. In Britain, the gauge was fixed at 4ft 8½in (1.435m) in the mid-1800s. Before then, the width of trains and gauges varied across networks. So a train from one rail network could not run over the lines of another.

Hard labour

Laying rail track is backbreaking work. Up until the mid-1900s, it was always done by hand. The ground is flattened first. Then crushed rock is laid to form a solid base before the sleepers are put into position. The rails rest on metal baseplates to hold them firm. The baseplates are secured to the sleepers either by spikes (big nails), track bolts or large metal spring-clips. Today, machines are used to lay track in most countries, although some countries still use manual labour.

MAKING TRACKS

You will need: two sheets of stiff card stock measuring 26x11cm/ 10¼x4¼in, pencil, ruler, scissors, glue and glue brush, silver and brown paint, paintbrush, water pot, one sheet of foam board measuring 13x20cm/8x5in, A4/11x8½in sheet of paper, masking tape, one sheet of thin card stock measuring 10x5cm/4x2in.

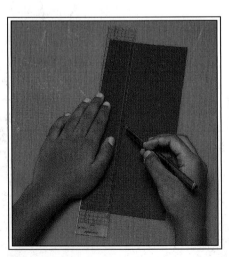

1 Place one large piece of card lengthways. Draw a line 1cm/⅜in in from each of the outside edges. Draw two lines, each 3.5cm/1⅜in in from the outside edges. This is side A.

2 Turn the card over (side B) and place it lengthways. Draw lines 4cm/1½in and 4.75cm/1¾in in from each edge. Repeat steps 1 and 2 with the second large piece of card.

3 Hold the ruler firmly against one of the lines you have drawn. Use the tip of a pair of scissors to score along the line. Repeat for all lines on both sides of both pieces of card.

4 Place the cards A side up. For each one in turn, fold firmly along the two pairs of outer lines. Fold up from the scored side. Turn the card over. Repeat for inner lines.

5 With the A side up, press the folds into the I-shape of the rail. Open out again. Glue the B side of the 2cm/¾in wide middle section as shown. Repeat for the second rail.

6 Give your two rails a metallic look by painting the upper (A) sides silver. Leave the paint to dry, then apply a second coat. Leave the second coat to dry.

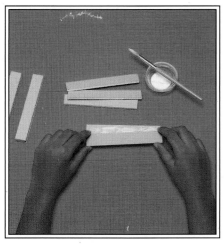

7 Use a pencil and ruler to mark out ten 13x2cm/5x¾in strips on the foam board. Cut them out. Glue two strips together to make five sleepers. Leave them to dry.

8 Paint the sleepers brown on their tops and sides to make them look like wood. Leave them to dry, then apply a second coat of paint. Leave the second coat to dry, too.

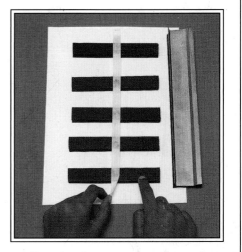

9 Lay the sleepers on a piece of paper, 3cm/1³⁄₆in apart. Hold them in place with a central strip of masking tape.

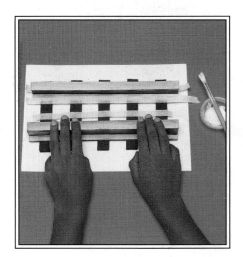

10 Glue the base of one rail and press it into place along the line of sleepers. The outside edge of the rail should be 1.5cm/⅝in in from the edge of the sleeper. Glue the other rail into position in the same way. Secure the rails in place with masking tape until the glue is dry. Then gently remove all masking tape.

11 Make at least two sets of rails. These will be able to carry the *Toy Train* and *Brake Van* described in later projects. To join the rails, roll up the short length of thin card. Insert one end into the top of the I-shape in one rail. Gently push the second rail on to the other end.

STEAMING AHEAD

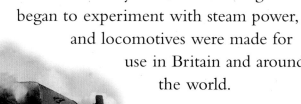

Horses, oxen or people provided the pulling power for carriages on rails and roads for thousands of years. In the 1800s, inventors came up with an alternative. They worked out how to use steam power for pulling wheeled vehicles. In 1825, the world's first public steam railway, the 40km/25 mile Stockton and Darlington line, opened in England. At its opening, the train hauled both freight and passenger carriages. Later, it was used mainly for carrying coal. Five years later, the Liverpool and Manchester line opened with steam-driven passenger trains. The company had run a competition called the Rainhill Trials to find the best locomotive. Both horse-drawn and steam locomotives took part. The steam-driven *Rocket* won.

The success of the *Rocket* convinced investors to back the development of steam-powered locomotives. The brains behind the *Rocket* and the Stockton and Darlington and the Liverpool and Manchester railways were George Stephenson and his son Robert. In 1823, they set up the world's first locomotive factory. Other British engineers began to experiment with steam power, and locomotives were made for use in Britain and around the world.

Race to success

The *Rocket,* designed and built by George and Robert Stephenson, convinced people that steam power was better than horse power. At the Rainhill Trials in 1829, the *Rocket* covered 112km/70 miles at an average speed of 24kmh/15mph.

Slow train to China

This Chinese locomotive is a KD class, which followed an American design. The Chinese did not make their own locomotives until they began to set up their own factories in the 1950s. Before then, locomotives had been imported from countries such as the USA, Britain and Japan. Some Chinese trains are still steam-driven today, although diesel and electric have replaced most of them.

hot gases pass
through to boiler

firebox

cab

*boiler tubes
surrounded by water*

regulator valve *engine*

*steam passes
through pipes
into cylinders*

chimney

smokebox

*steam
valve*

*piston inside
cylinder*

driving wheels

coupling rod

connecting rod

leading wheels

Steam traction

A steam engine converts the energy released from combustion into kinetic energy or movement. First, fuel (most often coal) is burned in a firebox to produce hot gases. The gases pass through boiler tubes that run the length of the water-filled boiler. The hot, gas-filled tubes heat the surrounding water and turn it into steam. This steam passes into cylinders, each of which contains a close-fitting piston. The steam pushes the piston along. The steam then escapes via a valve (one-way opening), and the piston can move back again. Rods connect the piston to the wheels. As the piston moves back and forth, it moves the rods, which, in turn, make the wheels go around.

FACT BOX
- Steam locomotives need 100 litres/26 gallons of water for every 1.6km/1 mile they travel. It takes 12–25kg/25–55lb of coal to turn the water into steam.

Big wheels

The Stirling Single locomotive had only one pair of large driving wheels. These were driven directly by the piston and connecting rod from the cylinder. Most steam locomotives had two or more pairs of driving wheels linked by coupling rods. The Single, designed by British engineer Patrick Stirling in the 1870s, reached speeds of 129kmh/80mph.

The Big Boys

In the 1940s, American engineers were designing huge steam locomotives such as this Union Pacific Challenger. At more than 40m/130ft, the Union Pacific's Big Boys were the world's longest-ever steam locomotives – more than five times the length of the Stephensons' *Rocket*. They could haul long passenger or freight trains speedily across the country's vast landscape.

BEARING THE LOAD

Staying power

The coupling rod that connects the driving wheel to the other wheels is the lowest of the three rods in this picture. The connecting rod just above links the driving wheel with the cylinder. To stop train wheels from slipping sideways and falling off the rails, there is a rim called the flange on the inside of each wheel. This is a little different from the wheels you will make in this project, which have two flanges so that they sit snugly on the model rails from the *Making Tracks* project.

THE VEHICLE and machinery carried by a modern locomotive's underframe and wheels may weigh over 100 tons. As bigger and more powerful locomotives were built, more wheels were added to carry the extra weight. Early steam locomotives had only two pairs of wheels. Most steam locomotives had two, three or four pairs of driving wheels, all of which turn in response to power from the cylinders. The cylinders house the pistons, whose movement pushes the driving wheels around via a connecting rod. The other wheels are connected to the driving wheel by a coupling rod, so that they turn at the same time. The small wheels in front of the driving wheels are called leading wheels. The ones behind are the trailing wheels. Locomotives are defined by the total number of wheels. For example, a 4-4-0 type locomotive has four leading, four driving and no trailing wheels.

MAKING AN UNDERFRAME

You will need: A2/22x17in sheet of stiff card stock, pencil, ruler, pair of compasses, scissors, glue and glue brush, masking tape, four 10cm/4in lengths of 0.5cm/³⁄₁₆in diameter dowel, four pieces of 5x5cm/2x2in thin card stock, silver and black paint, paintbrush, water pot, four map pins.

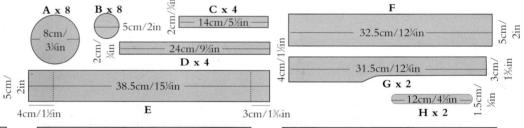

1 Draw and cut out the templates from the stiff card. Use a pair of compasses to draw the wheel templates A and B.

2 Roll the rim templates C and D into rings. Glue and tape to hold. Glue each small wheel circle on to either side of a small ring as shown. Repeat for big wheels. Leave to dry.

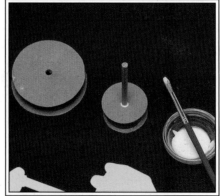

3 Use a pencil to enlarge the compass hole on one side of each wheel. Glue one end of each piece of dowel. Push the dowels into the holes of two big and two small wheels.

4 Roll the 5x5cm/2x2in card into sleeves to fit loosely over each piece of dowel. Tape to hold. Make wheel pairs by fixing the remaining wheels on to the dowel as in step 3.

5 When the glue is dry, paint all four pairs of wheels silver. You do not need to paint the dowel axles. Paint two coats, letting the first dry before you apply the second.

6 Use a ruler and pencil to mark eight equal segments on the outside of each wheel. Paint a small circle over the compass hole, and the middle of each segment black.

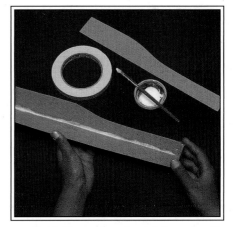

7 Fold along the dotted lines on E. Glue all three straight edges of template G and stick to template E. Repeat this for the other side. Secure all joins with masking tape.

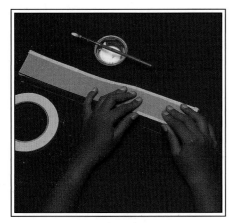

8 Glue the open edges of the underframe. Fit template F on top and hold until firm. Tape over the joins. Give the underframe two coats of black paint. Leave to dry.

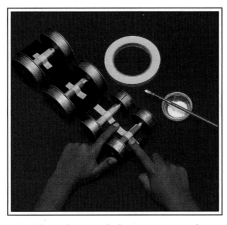

9 Glue the card sleeves on to the base of the underframe. Small wheel axles go 3cm/1³⁄₁₆in and 7cm/2¾in from the front, big wheels 3.5cm/1⅜in and 13cm/5in from the back. Tape to secure.

10 Give the coupling rods (H) two coats of silver paint. Let the paint dry between coats.

11 Press a map pin through each end of the coupling rods, about 0.5cm/³⁄₁₆in from edge. Press the pin into each big wheel about 1.5cm/⅝in beneath the middle.

12 The wheels on this underframe are arranged for a 4-4-0 type locomotive. You will be able to run the underframe along the model tracks you made in the *Making Tracks* project. The wheels will fit on the rails just like those of a real train. In real locomotives, however, the wheels are mounted on pivoting units called bogies, or trucks. When the train comes to a curve in the track, they move to allow the train to follow the curve. Each bogie has four to six wheels.

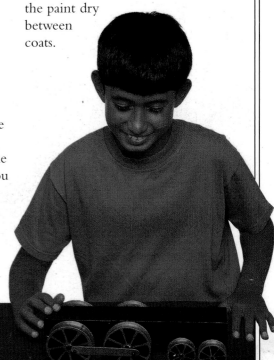

DIESEL AND ELECTRIC POWER

ODAY, MOST high-speed trains are either diesel, electric or a combination of the two. Diesel and electric trains are far more fuel-efficient, cost less to run and can stop or speed up more quickly than steam trains. Electric trains are also better for the environment, because they do not give off polluting exhaust fumes.

The first electric locomotive ran in 1879 at an exhibition in Berlin in Germany. However, it was another 20 or so years before rail companies began to introduce electric trains into regular service. Similarly, the first reliable diesel engine was demonstrated in 1889 by its inventor, the French-born German Rudolf Diesel. It took a further 25 years for railway engineers to design the first practical diesel locomotives. Diesel trains entered regular service during the 1920s in the USA, and during the 1930s in Britain. Steam locomotives were last used regularly in the USA in 1960, in 1968 in Britain and in 1977 in Germany.

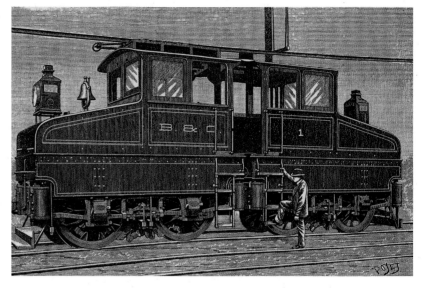

Electric pioneer
In 1895, the B&O *No. 1* became the world's first electric locomotive to run on a mainline railroad. It entered service in Baltimore in the USA (B&O is short for Baltimore and Ohio Railroad). The route of the B&O *No. 1* took it through many tunnels. One of the advantages of electric locomotives is that, unlike steam trains, they do not fill tunnels and carriages with steam and smoke.

Beautiful Bugattis
Racing-car designer Ettore Bugatti designed this diesel train for the French *État* and Paris Lyons *Méditerranée* railways. In the early 1930s, Bugatti's first trains were diesel- or petrol-driven single railcars (self-propelled passenger cars). Instead of being hauled by a locomotive, the railcar had its own engine. The railcar-and-carriage combination shown left was a later introduction. Bugatti came up with the train's streamlined shape by testing his designs in wind tunnels. In 1935, one of his trains reached 196kmh/122mph.

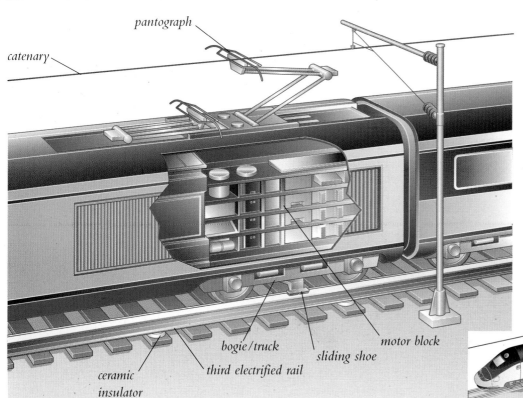

catenary

pantograph

bogie/truck

sliding shoe

motor block

third electrified rail

ceramic insulator

Picking up power

Electric locomotives are powered in one of two ways. Some draw electricity from a catenary (overhead cable). This is connected to the locomotive by an 'arm' called a pantograph on the roof. Others draw power from a third rail. The locomotive connects to the rail by a device called a shoe. The Eurostar trains that operate in Europe can use either power source depending on what country they are going through.

Long-distance runner

Until the late 1990s, CL class diesel-electric engines worked the long Indian Pacific route across the entire Australian continent. This railway runs between Perth, on the Indian Ocean, and Sydney, on the Pacific, a distance of over 4,300km/2,700 miles in 65 hours. The CL class were then replaced by Great Southern Rail's NR class diesel-electrics.

Dutch double decker

Dutch Railways' IRM (*InterRegio Materieel*) electric trains are double-decked to cater for high levels of traffic in the densely populated country. There are also self-powered multiple units (*Koplopers*) – *Plan Z* or *Intercity Materieel* – and the *Intercity Rijtuigen* or ICR locomotive-hauled carriages. The country's main passenger operator is NS, *Nederlandse Spoorwegen* (Dutch Railways).

Cisalpino Pendolino

In the 1990s, Italy developed a tilting train or pendolino, called the ETR (*Elletro Treni Rapidi*) 470 Cisalpino. These dual-voltage trains were operated by an Italian-Swiss consortium (group of companies). Services began in September 1996 between Italy and Switzerland. However, the 470 Cisalpinos suffered technical and reliability problems and were not successful. The next generation ETR 600 pendolinos, with a top speed of 250kmh/155mph entered service in 2008.

MAPPING THE RAILWAYS

Trains cannot easily climb mountains or cope with sharp corners. Planning and mapping the route of a railway is not a simple matter of drawing a straight line between two destinations. New routes have to be worked out carefully, so that difficult terrain is avoided, and time and money will not be wasted on tunnel- or bridge-building. Accurate maps are made before work starts to show every bend of the planned railway and the height of the land it will run through. Once construction starts, separate teams of workers may be building sections of track in different parts of the country. The maps are essential to make sure they are all following the same route and will join up when the separate parts meet.

Passengers do not need such detailed maps. They just need to find out which train to catch to get to the place they want to go. They do not need to know each curve or bridge along the way, just the names of the stations. Passenger maps provide a simplified version of the rail routes, or sometimes a diagram.

Railroads in the Wild West
You can see how the railroads often followed a similar route to the wagon trails, passing through mountain passes or river valleys. After the first east-to-west-coast railroad was completed (the Central Pacific Railroad joined the Union Pacific Railroad in 1869), people could cross the continent in just ten days.

Early American railroad
A train runs along the Mohawk and Hudson Railroad, New York State, in the USA. This railroad line opened in 1831 and was built to replace part of the 64km/40-mile route of the Erie Canal. This section of the canal had several locks, which caused delays to the barges. The journey took half the time it had taken by canal.

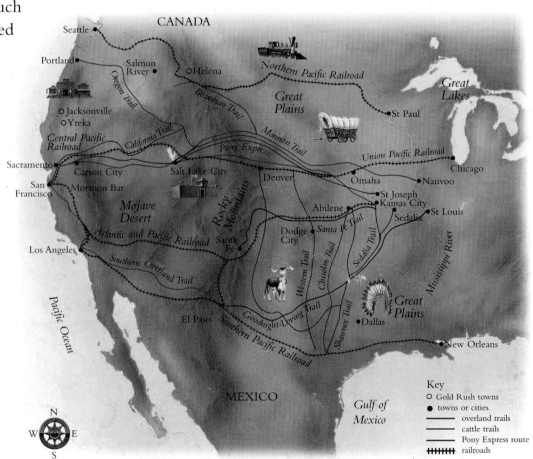

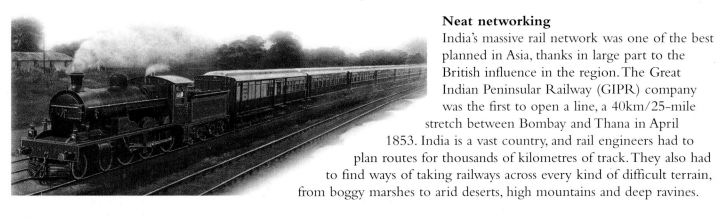

Neat networking

India's massive rail network was one of the best planned in Asia, thanks in large part to the British influence in the region. The Great Indian Peninsular Railway (GIPR) company was the first to open a line, a 40km/25-mile stretch between Bombay and Thana in April 1853. India is a vast country, and rail engineers had to plan routes for thousands of kilometres of track. They also had to find ways of taking railways across every kind of difficult terrain, from boggy marshes to arid deserts, high mountains and deep ravines.

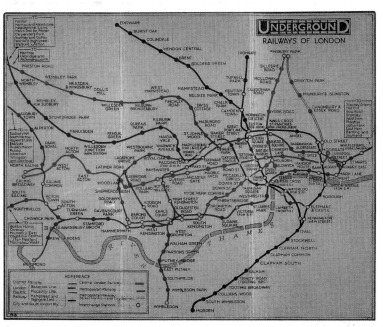

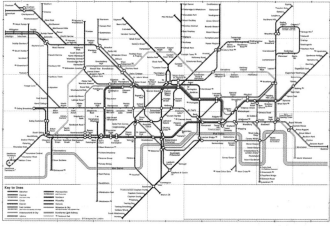

Designing ideas

Apart from the colour-coded routes, the 1927 map of the London Underground (at left) looks very different from a 21st-century version (shown above). Early route maps were hard to follow because they tried to show the real geographical route of lines. More abstract, diagrammatical maps were the brainwave of British engineering draughtsman Henry C. Beck. His 1933 redesign of the London Underground map is similar to electrical circuit diagrams and is still in use today. It makes no attempt to show the real geographical route and is not to scale.

Surveying railway lines

Today, computer programs are used to plan and design new railway routes. Data collected from on-the-ground surveying equipment (shown here), or the latest high-tech global positioning systems, is fed into a computer. The information is analysed to make sure that the new rail route is feasible. The most direct route is not always the cheapest. Surveyors must consider factors such as difficult terrain, environmental benefits and existing rail networks when planning new routes.

BUILDING RAILWAYS

THERE WERE NO automatic tools or building machines in the 1800s when the first railways were built. Everything was done by hand. Gangs of manual workers, called navvies in Britain, moved mountains of earth using nothing but picks, shovels and barrows. Horses pulled the heaviest loads. Never before had so much earth been shifted, or so many bridges or tunnels built.

The challenge for the engineers who planned the railways was to construct tracks that were as level as possible. In the early days, locomotives had difficulty climbing even the slightest slope.

Channels called cuttings were dug or blasted through low hills, while mounds of earth and rock were piled into embankments to carry tracks over boggy or low ground. Railway routes had to avoid crossing high mountains and deep valleys. Sometimes, though, there was no getting around these obstacles. In the late 1800s, engineers such as Isambard Kingdom Brunel in Britain and Gustave Eiffel in France, began to design tunnels and bridges that were longer and stronger than the world had ever known.

Army on the march

In the 1800s, railways were carved out of the landscape by workers called navigators, or navvies. Originally, navvies built navigations, or canals, equipped with little more than picks and shovels. Gangs of navvies often moved from place to place, as one track, tunnel or bridge was completed and work on a new one started up. Some of the workers lived in temporary camps, while others rented rooms in nearby towns. Navvies had strong muscles, but many were also skilled carpenters, miners, stonemasons or blacksmiths.

The best route

Millions of tons of earth and rock were blasted away for cuttings and to make rail routes as level and as straight as possible. Even modern trains slow down on hills. Early steam locomotives just ground to a halt. Sharp curves would cause trains to derail. Alfred Nobel's development of dynamite in 1866 made blasting safer. It was more stable than earlier explosives.

FACT BOX
• The Seikan Tunnel that links the Japanese islands of Hokkaido and Honshu is the deepest mainline rail tunnel in the world. The track level lies 100m/330ft beneath the seabed and 240m/790ft below sea level. It is also the longest undersea tunnel, though the Channel Tunnel between the UK and France has a longer undersea portion.

• At 13km/8 miles, the world's longest double-decker road and railway bridge system connects Japan's Honshu and Shikoku islands.

Bridging the valleys

There is not one perfect design for any bridge. In each case, a railway engineer has to take many factors into consideration before making the decision. These include the weight and frequency of traffic over the bridge, whether the underlying rock is hard or soft, the bridge's appearance in the landscape and the overall cost of the project.

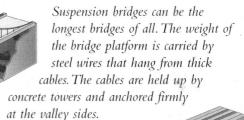

Suspension bridges can be the longest bridges of all. The weight of the bridge platform is carried by steel wires that hang from thick cables. The cables are held up by concrete towers and anchored firmly at the valley sides.

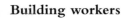

The beam bridge is made up of a horizontal platform supported on two or more piers (pillars). Sometimes a framework of steel girders is added. The girders act as a brace to strengthen and support the beam bridge between its piers.

The arch bridge can be built over very steep valleys or fast-flowing rivers, where it would be difficult to build piers. Steel or reinforced concrete supports press towards each other in the arch shape, making a very strong base for the bridge platform.

Building workers

Thousands of skilled workers are involved in the manufacture of locomotives and rolling stock – passenger carriages and freight wagons. There are whole factories that specialize in making particular parts such as buffers or electric motors. At this factory, wheels and axles are being put together to be fitted to the bogie (truck). Today, much of the work is carried out by machines, but some tasks, such as precision welding (joining of metal parts), still have to be done by hand.

Machines lighten the load

A Paved Concrete Track (PACT for short) machine is one way of taking the sweat out of laying railway track. It lays a trackbed of continuous concrete. Then, when the concrete is dry, other machines lift and clip the metal rails on top. In another automated method of track-laying, complete sections of track are made in factories with the rails already fixed to concrete sleepers (ties). They are then transported to the site and lifted into position by cranes. Machines that could do such jobs automatically were introduced in the mid–1900s. They allowed the work to be done much more quickly, involving fewer people and a lot less effort.

LOAD-BEARING TUNNEL

TUNNELS OFTEN have to bear the weight of millions of tons of rocks and earth – or even water – above. One way of preventing the tunnel from collapsing is to make a continuous brick arch run along the length of the tunnel. Wedge-shaped keystones at the peak of the arch lock the whole structure together and support the arch and everything else above it. An arched roof is much stronger than a flat roof, because any weight above the tunnel is passed down through the sides of the arch and out towards the ground.

Between 1871 and 1881, a 15km/9-mile long tunnel was driven through Europe's highest mountains, the Alps, to link Switzerland to northern Italy. The Gotthard tunnel was the greatest achievement in tunnel engineering of the time. More recently, TBMs (tunnel-boring machines) are used, such as for the Channel Tunnel. A big drill carves out the hole, sending the spoil backwards on a conveyor belt. Behind it, robotic cranes lift pre-cast concrete sections of the tunnel into place.

Keystone is key
Before a tunnel is built, engineers have to make sure the rock and soil are easy to cut through but firm enough not to collapse. A framework is used to build brick arches. The bricks are laid around both sides of the framework up towards the middle. When the central keystone is in place, the arch will support itself and the framework can be removed.

SUPPORTING ARCH

You will need: two wooden building blocks or house bricks, two pieces of thick cardboard (width roughly the same as the length of the blocks or bricks), a few heavy pebbles.

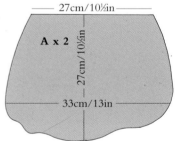

— 27cm/10½in —
A x 2
27cm/10½in
33cm/13in

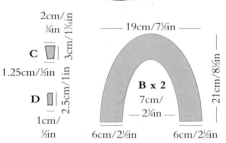

2cm/ ¾in
3cm/1⅛in
C
1.25cm/½in
1cm
2.5cm/1in
D
1cm/ ½in

— 19cm/7½in —
B x 2
7cm/ 2¾in
21cm/8⅜in
6cm/2½in   6cm/2½in

KEYSTONE

You will need: masking tape, thick cardboard 46x27cm/18x10½in, two sheets of thick cardboard 36x30cm/14¼x12in, ruler, pencil, scissors, thin card stock 44x40cm/17¼x16in, newspaper, 115g/4oz/1 cup of flour, 120ml/4fl oz/½ cup of water, acrylic paints, paintbrush, water pot, A4/11x8½in sheet of thin card stock, glue and glue brush.

1 Place one of the pieces of cardboard on top of the building blocks. Place pebbles on top as shown above. You will see that the tunnel roof sags under the weight.

2 Curve a second piece of cardboard under the flat roof as shown. The roof supports the weight of the pebbles because the arch supports the flat section.

1 Tear off about four long strips of masking tape. Curve the 46x27cm/18x10½in cardboard lengthways. Use the tape to hold the curve in place as shown above.

2 Copy the two templates A on to two 36x30cm/14¼x12in pieces of cardboard. Cut out the shapes. Attach each one to the sides of the tunnel and secure with tape.

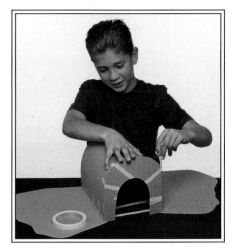

3 Fold the 44x40cm/17¼x16in thin card in half. Copy the arch template B on to it. Cut out to make two entrances. Stick these to the tunnel with masking tape.

4 Scrunch newspaper into balls and tape to the tunnel and landscape. Mix the flour and water to make a thick paste. Dip newspaper strips in the paste. Layer them over the tunnel.

5 Leave to dry. When completely dry and hard, remove the tape and paint the tunnel and landscape green. Apply three coats, letting each one dry before you apply the next.

6 Paint the thin card to look like bricks. Draw and cut out templates C and D. Draw around C to make two keystones and D to make lots of bricks. Carefully cut out the shapes.

7 When the paint is dry, glue each keystone at the very top of each tunnel entrance. Then glue bricks around the arch either side of the keystone as shown. In a real tunnel, there would have been lots of central keystones running along the length of the tunnel.

8 Add finishing touches to your model using brown and green paints. Scrunch up newspaper into balls and dip them in the paste to make fake bushes. Leave them to dry and then paint them with brown and green paints. Do at least two or three coats. Leave them to dry between coats.

STATION STOP

ONCE PASSENGER trains began running in the 1830s, people needed special buildings where they could buy tickets and shelter from the weather while they waited to board. No one had ever designed or built railway stations before. The owners of the new railway companies wanted to make as much money as possible, so they had big, impressive mainline stations built to attract customers. Long platforms were essential for trains with many carriages, so that passengers could get on and off trains safely. There also had to be waiting rooms and restaurants, as well as offices where staff worked.

London's Euston Station was the first to have separate platforms for arrivals and departures. This station was also among the earliest to have a metal and glass roof over the platforms. Euston was opened in 1838. From then on, most big stations had glass and metal roofs. They were relatively cheap and easy to build, and they also let in a lot of daylight, which helped to save money on artificial lighting. In those days, lighting was provided by expensive gas lamps.

Housed in style
An early steam train puffs out of the first circular engine shed, built in 1847 in London. Even the engine sheds where steam locomotives were housed for maintenance or repair were well designed. In the middle of these circular sheds was a turntable with short sections of track arranged around it, rather like the spokes of a wheel. Locomotives were parked on each section of track and released when they were needed for a journey.

Decorative ironwork
The iron pillars of stations in the 1900s were cast into a fantastic variety of shapes and then beautifully painted. At this time, cast iron was one of the latest building materials. Cast-iron pillars and arches were fairly cheap and quick to erect, as well as being a strong framework for station walls and roofs.

Temples of fashion
Bristol Temple Meads Station, England, looked like this in the 1800s. Engineers and architects tried to make their stations look stylish as well as be functional. During the 1800s, it was fashionable to copy the great building styles of the past. Bristol Temple Meads Station imitated the magnificent Gothic cathedrals and churches of medieval times. Small country stations, on the other hand, often looked like cottages or suburban villas.

Classical station

The main station building of Washington Union Station in the USA is typical of stations built in the early 1900s. It has a lofty vaulted ceiling and interiors made of wooden panels. It was opened in 1907 and was built by the Washington Terminal Company, which was specially formed by railroads serving the city.

German hub

Busy Cologne *Hauptbahnhof* (main station) is at the heart of Germany's vast rail network in the north-west of the country. The old steel-and-glass train shed was damaged during World War II (1939–45) but was later rebuilt. In 2000, a new complex of shops, eateries and offices was incorporated into the structure.

Simple fare

Unlike the grand stations that serve cities, country stations are often very basic, such as this one at Pargothan, India. There are no platforms, and passengers climb into the trains from the track.

Single span

Atocha is the terminus of Spain's *Alta Velocita Española* (AVE) high-speed rail link between the capital, Madrid, and Seville in southern Spain. It was built in the early 1890s, and it serves all routes to the south, east and south-east of Madrid. The old single-span-roof main hall is now a tropical 'forest' with exotic plants.

FACT BOX

• The station with the most platforms is Grand Central Terminal in New York City, USA, which has 44 platforms connected to more than 65 railroad tracks on two levels.

• The world's highest station is Tanggula Railway Station in Tibet. It is at an altitude of 5,068m/16,627ft, over 500m/1,640ft higher than the Matterhorn in the Alps.

• In terms of passenger numbers, the world's busiest station is probably Shinjuku Station in Tokyo, Japan. It is used by almost four million people per day – it's difficult to count them all exactly!

SHRINKING WORLD

Ticket to ride
Cheap, speedy trains meant that for the first time ordinary people, rather than the wealthy, could travel for pleasure. Train companies began offering day-excursion trips in the early 1830s. Outings to the seaside were particularly popular.

Ceremonial spike
On 10 May 1869, a golden spike was hammered into the track when the world's first transcontinental railroad was completed, linking the east and west coasts of America. It was built by two companies, and the spike marked the meeting place of the two tracks at Promontory Summit in Utah.

Before the coming of the railways, the fastest way to travel was on horseback. Even though the swiftest racehorse can gallop at more than 60kmh/37mph, it cannot keep this speed up for longer than a few minutes. Trains, on the other hand, can travel at high speed for hours on end. They can also transport hundreds of people at a time, or tens of wagon-loads of freight, across vast distances. As more and more railway lines began snaking across the countryside, life speeded up and the world seemed to grow smaller. People and goods could reach new places.

During the 1800s, rail technology spread from Britain all over the world. Tracks were laid between towns and cities at first. Later, railways slowly grew to link countries and span continents. The world's first transcontinental railroad was completed in the USA in 1869. The expansion of the rail system there was rapid. Railways were built through areas that had not yet been settled and played an important part in opening up many parts of the country.

FACT BOX
• With around 225,000km/ 140,000 miles of track, the USA has the world's longest rail network – enough to wrap around the Equator five times.

• It would take you just over eight days to ride the entire length of the world's longest railway, the Trans-Siberian from Moscow to Vladivostok. Opened in 1903, it runs for 9,289km/5,772 miles and crosses eight time zones.

Desert runner
When surveyors planned the western section of Australia's transcontinental railway, they plotted what is still the world's longest stretch of straight track. This 478km/297–mile section lies within a vast, treeless desert called the Nullarbor Plain between Port Augusta and Kalgoorlie in southwestern Australia. The western section of this railway opened in 1917. Then it was relaid in 1969 to avoid soil settlement problems and also to make the different rail gauges in different Australian states the same.

Ruling by rail

A steam train passes over a bridge in India. During the 1800s, the British gradually introduced rail networks to India and other countries in the British Empire. By speeding up the movement of government officials and the military, trains helped Britain keep control of its empire. Trade goods could be moved more quickly, too, which benefited British-owned companies. By 1939, the country had more than 50,000km/ 31,000 miles of track.

Keeping up with the times

The time in any place in the world is calculated from Greenwich Mean Time, which is the local time at 0 degrees longitude at Greenwich in London, England. Local time in other countries is calculated as behind or in front of Greenwich Mean Time. Before the railways, even cities within the same country kept their own local time, and accurate timetables were impossible. Time-keeping had to be standardized if people were to know when to catch their trains. British railway companies standardized time-keeping using Greenwich Mean Time in 1847.

Cross-Canada challenge

Passenger trains can today make the original spectacular 4,650km/2,890-mile journey across most of Canada, from Vancouver to Montréal, in three days. When the first Canadian Pacific railway was completed in 1887, the trip took steam trains about a week. The biggest challenge for the army of workers who built the railway was taking the track through the Rocky Mountains – at Kicking Horse Pass, it climbs to 1,624m/5,328ft.

A PASSION FOR TRAINS

In 1830, a young British actress, Fanny Kemble, wrote to a friend about her journey pulled by a "brave little she-dragon … the magical machine with its wonderful flying white breath and rhythmical unvarying pace".

Over the years, all sorts of people – young and old, male and female, rich and poor – have caught Fanny's enthusiasm for trains. Some people love riding on them, enjoying the scenery flickering past the windows and chatting to the strangers they meet on the journey. Others are happiest when they are standing at the end of a platform, spotting trains and noting down locomotive numbers. Other enthusiasts spend their spare time building their own private museum of rail history. They collect anything from old railway tickets, timetables and luggage labels, to early signal equipment, station clocks and locomotive numberplates. Some people 'collect' journeys and take pride in experiencing some of the world's most famous railways.

Museum piece

You can still ride a real steam train today, although in most countries only where short stretches of line have been preserved. Many classic locomotives are on display in railway museums. Visitors can usually get close enough to touch, and sometimes they are allowed to climb up inside the cab. You should never get this close when spotting working trains, however. Always stand well back on the platform, and never climb down on to the track.

Railway mania

The walls of this railway enthusiast's room are decorated with prizes collected during years of hunting through junk stores and car-boot sales, and attending auctions. Lamps and many other pieces of railway and station equipment came on to the market in Britain during the 1960s, when the government closed down hundreds of the country's least-used stations and branch lines.

Collecting signals

During the late 1900s, many old semaphore signals like these were made redundant. They were replaced with light signals controlled from power signal boxes. Many of the old signals were purchased by Britain's heritage railways, but a few rail enthusiasts bought signals for their gardens. The ones in this picture are Great Western Railway design signals, dating from the 1940s.

Museum pieces

The Baltimore and Ohio Museum was set up in the city of Baltimore by the Baltimore and Ohio Railroad in 1953. The main exhibits are displayed in a full-circle roundhouse in what used to be the railroad's workshops. The exhibits feature a full range of locomotives from the last 180 years. They include a replica of the first American steam locomotive of 1829 and a recently retired diesel locomotive.

Tickets, please

Rail tickets and timetables are all collectable items for those who are interested in trains and train journeys. A trainspotter's handbook and a set of railway timetables are essential equipment for the serious enthusiast. You can buy handbooks at specialist bookshops. They list all the working locomotives in a particular country.

WARNING BOX

• Never go trainspotting without first asking your parents' permission and telling them where you are going.
• At stations, always stand well back from the platform edge.
• Railway lines often have fences on either side to keep people a safe distance from the track. Stand behind the fence – never climb over it.
• Modern trains are fast and make very little noise. If you disregard these simple rules, you will be risking your life.

Number crunching

Locomotives have number plates in much the same way that cars do. The plate is usually on the front of the engine. Unlike a car's registration plate, however, some train number plates have no letters on them. Trainspotters aim to collect the number of every working locomotive, but with so many locomotives in operation, it is a very time-consuming hobby.

TRAINS IN MINIATURE

ODEL TRAINS are just about as old as steam locomotives. The first ones were not for children, though. They were made for the locomotive manufacturers of the early 1800s to show how the newly invented, full-sized machines worked.

Although most toy trains are miniature versions of the real thing, they come in different scales or sizes. Most are built in O scale, which is ⅟₄₈th the size of the real train. The smallest are Z scale, which is ⅟₂₂₀th the size of a real train. Z-scale locomotives are small enough to fit inside a matchbox. It is extremely difficult to make accurate models to this small a scale, so Z-scale train sets are usually the hardest to find in stores and the most expensive to buy.

All the exterior working parts of the original are shown on the best model locomotives, from the chimney on top of the engine to the coupling and connecting rods.

Smile, please
In the early 1900s, a few lucky children owned their own toy train. Some early toy trains had clockwork motors or tiny steam engines. Others were 'carpet-runners'. These were simply pushed or pulled along the floor.

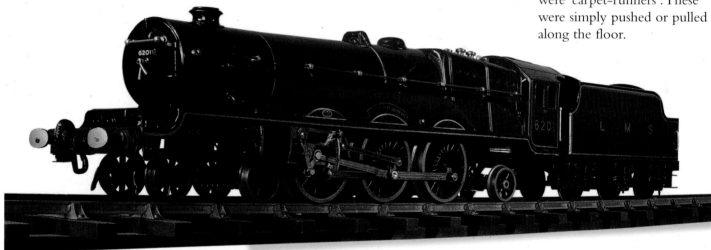

Top-class toys
One British manufacturer of model trains was Bassett-Lowke, the maker of this fine model of *Princess Elizabeth*. Another manufacturer was Hornby, whose trains first went on sale in the 1920s. Hornby quickly grew into Britain's most popular model. Lionel is probably the leading manufacturer of miniature trains in the USA. All produced many different models of real-life trains.

A model world
In the 1920s, toymakers started producing small-scale table-top model railways. Stations and track took up less space than older, larger-scale models. Many of these models were electric-powered and made from cast metal and tinplate by the German firm Bing. Today, these models are very valuable.

The German connection

Model trains are being made at the Fleischmann Train Factory, Nuremberg, Germany. Fleischmann produces highly detailed models of the full range of modern European trains. Like earlier model-railway manufacturers, Fleischmann does not only make the trains. Collectors and model-railway enthusiasts can also buy everything that goes to make up a railway, including signals and signal boxes, lights and level crossings, engine sheds, bridges and tunnels. There are even stations and platforms with miniature newspaper kiosks, station staff and passengers.

Model behaviour

In the earliest train sets, miniature locomotives hauled wagons and carriages on a never-ending journey around a circular track. Gradually, toymakers began selling more complex layouts, with several sets of track linked by points (switches). Trains could switch from one track to another, just as in real railways.

Ticket to ride

Model trains come in all sizes, including those that are large enough for children and adults to ride on. These miniature trains have all the working parts of their full-sized parents, including a tiny firebox which the driver stokes with coal to keep the train chuffing along. In the USA in the late 1890s, small-gauge lines were appearing at showgrounds and in amusement parks. By the 1920s, longer miniature railways were being built in Britain and Germany. Today, many theme parks feature a miniature railway.

MODEL LOCOMOTIVES

A precision toy

As manufacturing techniques improved, so toy trains became increasingly sophisticated. Today, accurate, working, scale models have all the features of full-size working trains.

T OY TRAINS started to go on sale in the mid-1800s. Early toy trains were made of brightly painted wood, and often had a wooden track to run along. Soon, metal trains went on sale, many of them made from tinplate (thin sheets of iron or steel coated with tin). Some of these metal toys had wind-up clockwork motors. Clockwork toy trains were first sold in the USA during the 1880s. The most sophisticated models were steam-powered, with tiny engines fired by methylated-spirit (denatured alcohol) burners. Later they were powered by electric motors.

Railway companies often devised special design schemes, called liveries, for their locomotives and carriages. Steam locomotives had brass and copper decoration, and some also carried the company's logo or badge. Many toy trains are also painted in the livery of a real company.

TOY TRAIN

You will need:
26x26cm/10¼x10¼in card stock, masking tape, scissors, ruler, pencil, 10x10cm/4x4in card stock, glue and glue brush, card stock for templates, paints, paintbrush, water pot, underframe from earlier project, two push pins, 1x1cm/4½x½in red card stock, split pin.

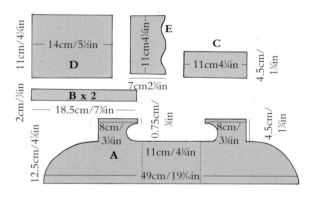

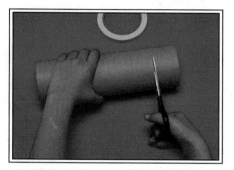

1 Roll the large card into an 8cm/3⅛in diameter tube. Secure it with masking tape. Cut a 6cm/2½in slit, 5cm/2in from one end.

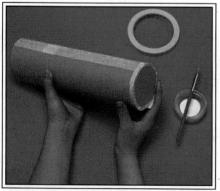

2 Hold the tube upright on the smaller piece of card. Draw around it. Cut this circle out. Glue the circle to the tube end farthest away from the slit. Tape to secure.

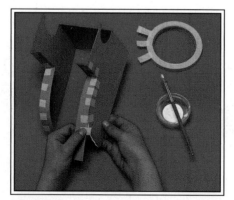

3 Copy and cut out templates. Fold template A along the dotted lines. Fold templates B across, 4.5cm/1⅜in from one end. Glue both strips to the cab as shown and secure with tape.

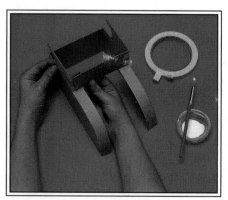

4 When the glue is dry, gently peel off the masking tape. Now glue on template C as shown above. Hold it in place with masking tape until the glue dries.

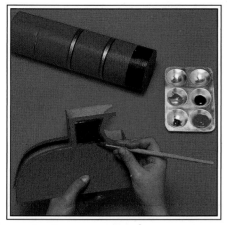

5 Apply two coats of green paint to the outside of the locomotive. Let the first coat dry before applying the second. Then paint the black parts. Add the red and gold last.

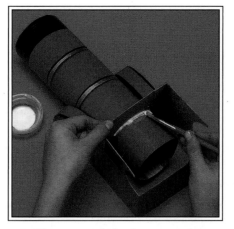

6 Glue around the bottom edge of the cab front C. Put a little glue over the slit in the tube. Fit the front of the cab into the slit. Leave the locomotive to one side to dry.

7 Give roof template D two coats of black paint. Let the paint dry between coats. Glue the top edges of the cab, and place the black roof on top. Leave until dry and firm.

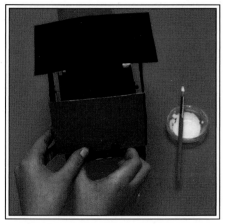

8 Glue the bottom of the cylindrical part of the train to the underframe you made in the *Underframe* project. Push pins into back of the cab and underframe.

9 Glue both sides of one end of the red strip. Slot this between the underframe and the cab, between the push pins. When firm, fold the strip and insert the split pin.

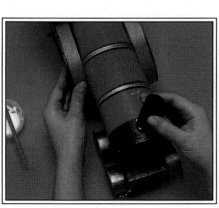

10 Paint one side of template E black. When dry, roll into a tube and secure with masking tape. Glue wavy edge and secure to front of locomotive as shown above.

The shape of the locomotive in this project has a cab typical of the real versions made in the 1910s. Just like a real locomotive, the livery of your model train has been enhanced with red, black and gold decoration. The locomotive is now ready to run on the railway line you made in the Making Tracks project. The driver and fireman would have shared the cab of the locomotive. The driver controlled the speed of the train, following the signals and track speed restrictions. The fireman made sure of a good supply of steam by stoking the fire and filling the boiler with water.

SIGNALS AND SWITCHES

Hand signals
The first people to be responsible for train safety in Britain were the railway police. They used flags and lamps to direct the movements of trains. In the absence of flags, signals were given by hand. One arm outstretched horizontally meant "line clear", one arm raised meant "caution" and both arms raised meant "danger, stop".

THE EARLIEST railways were single tracks that ran directly between two places. Later, more tracks were laid and branched off these main lines. Trains could cross from one line to another on movable sections of track called points, or switches.

To avoid crashes, a system of signals was needed to show drivers if the track ahead was clear. The first signallers stood beside the track and waved flags during daylight or lamps at night. From 1841, human signallers were replaced by signals called semaphores on posts with wooden arms.

By 1889, three basics of rail safety were established by law in Britain – block, brake and lock. Block involved stopping a train until the one in front had passed by. Brakes are an obvious safety feature on passenger trains. Lock meant that points and signals had to be interlocked, so that a lever in the signal box could not be pulled without changing both the point and the signal.

Lighting up the night
Electric signals were not used until the 1920s, when colour-light signals were introduced. These signals look like road traffic lights. A green light means the track is clear, red shows danger and yellow means caution. Electric-light signals, such as these in France, are accompanied by displays showing the number of the signal, speed restrictions and other information for train drivers.

Mechanical signals
A railway policeman operates a Great Western Railway disc and crossbar signal. The disc and crossbar were at right angles and rotated so the driver could either see the full face of the disc, meaning "go", or the crossbar, meaning "stop".

Signal improvements

This hand-operated signal frame features details dating from the 1850s, when a signal system called interlocking was introduced. Signals and points were interlocked (linked) so that a single lever moved a signal and the set of points it protected at the same time. Levers in signal boxes or towers were moved by hand to set signals and points. In many countries today, signals are set automatically by computers in a central control room.

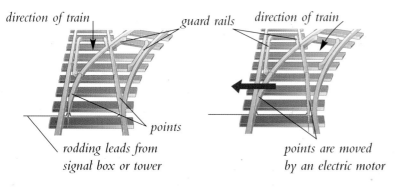

direction of train   *guard rails*   *direction of train*

points

rodding leads from signal box or tower

points are moved by an electric motor

Safety first

Semaphore signals such as these made a major difference to railway safety when they were introduced during the 1840s. At first, rail companies throughout the world used semaphore signals with oil lamps behind tinted glass to show at night whether the track was clear (green light) or at danger (red light). From the 1920s, many countries upgraded their systems by introducing electric-light signals.

Switching at the humpyard

Trains are switched from one track to another using points. Part of the track, called the blade, moves to guide the wheels smoothly from one route on to the other. It moves as a result of a signaller pulling a lever in the signal box or tower. The blade and lever are connected by a system of metal rods, and the lever cannot be pulled unless the signal is clear. From the late 1800s, rail companies built humpyards. These made it easier to shunt freight wagons together to make a train. As the wagons went over a hump in the yard, they uncoupled. When they went down the hump, they could be switched into different sidings using a set of points.

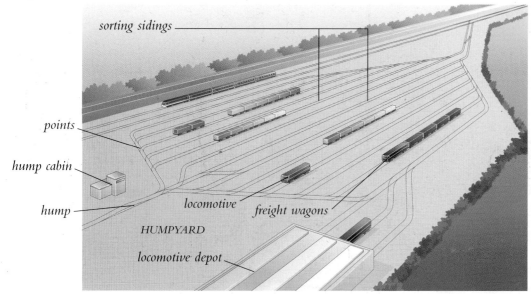

sorting sidings

points

hump cabin

hump

locomotive

freight wagons

HUMPYARD

locomotive depot

SAFETY FIRST

ACCIDENTS ARE a tragic feature of rail travel, but trains remain the safest form of land transport in most countries. Modern technology is largely responsible for the improvements in rail safety. In Britain, trains are fitted with an Automatic Warning System (AWS). If the signal indicates that the track ahead is clear, electric magnets between the rails send a message to equipment under the train. This causes a bell to sound in the driver's cab. If the signal is not clear, the magnet stays 'dead' and a horn sounds in the cab. If the driver does not react, the brakes come on automatically. An improved system, called Train Protection and Warning System (TPWS), uses existing AWS but also provides an automatic stop at a red signal and a speed trap in advance of the signal. A more advanced system is Automatic Train Protection (ATP). The train picks up electronic messages from the track, and they tell the driver to slow down or stop. If he or she fails to respond, there is a warning and the brakes come on. ATP also slows or stops the train if it exceeds the speed limit.

On collision course

Head-on crashes were more common in the early days of rail, even though there were far fewer trains. On some routes, there was only a single-track line. A train heading towards a station was in danger of meeting another train leaving it. In most countries today, trains are timetabled so that no two are on the same line at the same time. This situation arises only if a train passes a stop signal at a set of points.

Japanese crash

A crane lifts a derailed train along the Hanshin Railway near Shinzaike Station. The accident was caused by an earthquake that devastated the city of Kobe on the Japanese island of Honshu in 1995. Several stations and many kilometres of elevated railway lines were destroyed on the three main lines that run from Kobe.

All under control

From the 1960s, signalling over large areas has been controlled from centralized signal boxes or towers. They contain a control panel that displays all the routes, signals and points that the signal box controls. Signallers set up safe routes for trains in the area by operating switches and buttons. Signals work automatically, and the points change using electronic controls. This makes sure that trains cannot get on routes where there is an oncoming train. In the most modern signal control rooms, the routes appear on computer screens. Instead of pressing buttons or switches, the signaller uses a cursor to set up routes.

Tube stop

The driving controls of a London Underground, or 'Tube', train include a number of safety features. The red joystick is the traction brake controller, a manual control for the train's speed. This incorporates a 'dead man's handle', which means it must be held constantly by the driver in order for the train to move. The big red button is the emergency stop plunger.

Onboard safety

In the event of an emergency, passengers will always find standard safety devices, such as fire extinguishers and first-aid kits, on board a train.

Buffer zone

Buffers stop trains at the end of a line. They are made of metal or wood and metal and are fixed to the track. They are strong enough to absorb much of the energy of a colliding train. Signals control a train's speed so that even if a train collides with the bufferstops, it is usually moving slowly.

BRAKE VAN

Coupling up

A locomotive is joined to a wagon by a connection called a coupling. At first, chains or rigid bars were used to join carriages. Later, a rigid hook at the end of one vehicle connected to chains on the front of the next. From the late 1800s, couplings made from steel castings and springs were used, but uncoupling was done by hand. Today, passenger trains couple and uncouple automatically.

FEW EARLY steam locomotives had brakes. If the driver needed to stop quickly, he had to throw the engine into reverse. By the early 1860s, braking systems had been invented. Some passenger carriages also had their own handbrakes, operated by the train guards, or conductors. A brake van, or caboose, was added to the back of trains, too, but its brakes were operated by a guard riding inside.

The problem was that the train driver had no control over the rest of the train. If he wanted to stop, he had to blow the whistle to warn the guards to apply their brakes. The brakes on a locomotive and its carriages or wagons needed to be linked. This was made possible by the invention of an air-braking system in 1869. When the driver applies the brakes, compressed air travels along pipes linking all parts of the train and presses brake shoes. Air brakes are now used on nearly all railways.

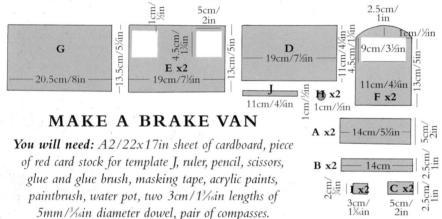

MAKE A BRAKE VAN

You will need: *A2/22x17in sheet of cardboard, piece of red card stock for template J, ruler, pencil, scissors, glue and glue brush, masking tape, acrylic paints, paintbrush, water pot, two 3cm/1³⁄₁₆in lengths of 5mm/³⁄₁₆in diameter dowel, pair of compasses.*

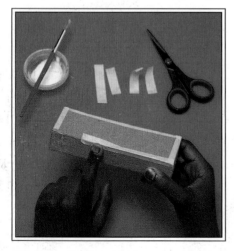

1 Copy the templates on to cardboard and cut them out. Glue templates A, B and C together to make the underframe as shown. Tape over the joins to secure them.

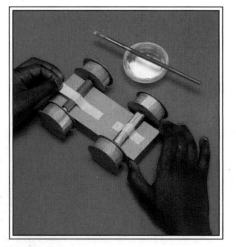

2 Make and paint two pairs of small wheels (diameter 5cm/2in) as in steps 1–5 in the *Underframe* project. Glue and tape the wheel pairs to the underframe.

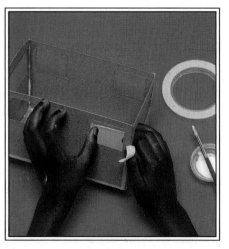

3 Glue the bottom edges of the van sides (E) to the van base (D). Then glue on the van ends (F). Secure the joins with masking tape until the glue is dry.

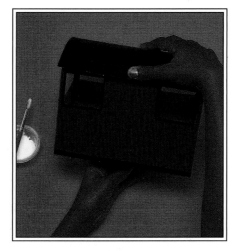

4 Paint the brake van brown with black details and the wheels and underframe black and silver. Apply two coats of paint, letting each one dry between coats.

5 Paint one side of template G black. Let the paint dry before applying a second coat. Glue the top edges of the van. Bend the roof to fit on the top of the van as shown.

6 Apply glue to the top surface of the underframe. Stick the brake van centrally on top. Press together until the glue holds firm. Leave to dry completely.

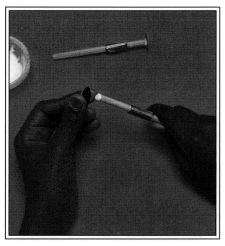

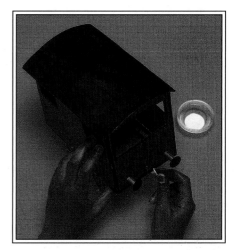

7 Roll up templates I into two 2cm/¾in tubes to fit loosely over the dowel. Tape to hold and paint them silver. Paint the buffer templates H black and stick on each dowel.

8 Use compasses to pierce two holes 2.5cm/1in from each side of the van and 1.5cm/⅝in up. Enlarge the holes with a pencil. Glue the end of each dowel buffer. Slot it into the hole. Leave to dry.

9 Cut a slot between the buffers. Fold red card template J in half. Glue each end to form a loop. Push the closed end into the slot. Hold it in place until the glue dries.

The brake van will also run on the tracks you made in the Making Tracks *project. You can join the red-card coupling to join the brake van to the model locomotive you made in the* Toy Train *project. On old-style trains, the brake van was at the back so that the guard could make sure that all the carriages stayed coupled. The brake van had one of two brake systems. One had hand-operated brakes that worked on the tread of the brake van's wheels. The other had a valve that allowed the guard to apply air brakes to all vehicles in the train.*

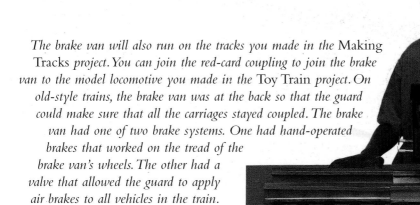

HAULING FREIGHT

Most of the traffic on the world's railways is made up of freight trains that transport goods such as coal and iron ore from mines and cloth and other manufactured goods from factories. The earliest freight trains were slow because they did not have effective braking systems. Technical developments now mean that freight trains can run much faster than before.

Freight trains made a vast difference to everyday life as the rail networks expanded and brought the country nearer to the city. For the first time, fresh food could be delivered quickly from country farms to city markets. People could also afford to heat their homes. The price of coal for household fires came down because moving coal by train was cheaper and faster than by horse-drawn carts or canal.

In the mid–1900s, motor vehicles and aircraft offered an alternative way of transporting freight. However, concerns about congestion and the environment mean that freight trains continue to be the cheapest, quickest and most environmentally friendly way of hauling a large volume of freight overland.

Four-legged freight service
The world's first public railway opened in 1803 – for horse-drawn freight wagons. The Surrey Iron Railway ran for a little more than 13km/8 miles between Wandsworth and Croydon near London. It went past a number of mills and factories. The factory owners paid a toll to use the railway and supplied their own horses and wagons.

Rolling stock
Freight wagons were ramshackle affairs when the first steam trains began running during the 1820s and 1830s. They had metal wheels but, unlike locomotives, they were mainly built from wood. Their design was based on the horse-drawn carts or coal wagons they were replacing. Waterproof tarpaulins were tied over goods to protect them from the weather.

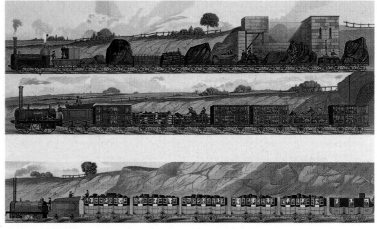

Slow but steady
In the early 1800s, the first steam locomotives hauled coal wagons called chaldrons from collieries to ships on nearby rivers. The locomotives were not very powerful. They could pull only a few wagons at a time. Going any faster would have been dangerous because neither the locomotives nor the wagons had much in the way of brakes.

Mail by rail

Railways first carried mail in the 1830s. A special mail carriage was introduced in Britain in 1838. Workers on board sorted the mail for delivery while the train was moving. These TPOs (travelling post offices) or mail rooms were phased out in 2004.

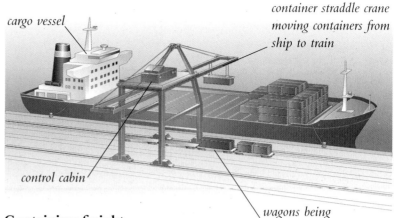

cargo vessel

container straddle crane moving containers from ship to train

control cabin

wagons being loaded with containers

Containing freight

From the 1960s, metal containers like giant boxes have transported goods by sea, rail and road. They are a way of combining different methods of transporting goods in the most effective way possible. The containers are simply lifted from one vehicle to another using large cranes called straddle cranes. The trains usually have specially designed flat wagons on to which the containers are locked into position. The containers remain sealed, apart from when they are inspected by customs officials.

Bulk transportation

Today, freight trains mainly transport heavy, bulky loads such as coal, iron ore, grain or building materials. Smaller, lighter goods are usually sent by road or air. Rail companies pioneered the idea of specially designed vehicles for different types of freight – tankers for liquids such as milk or chemicals, for example, and hoppers that tip sideways for unloading gravel or coal.

FACT BOX

• Today, freight trains haul bulky loads in purpose-built wagons.

• As many as 10,000 freight trains criss-cross the USA every day.

• Some of the world's freight trains have 200 wagons and can be up to 4km/2½ miles long.

• Modern diesel and electric trains can haul heavy loads at speeds of up to 120kmh/75mph.

Chinese circle

From the mid-1900s, Chinese electric locomotives hauled ore hoppers. The trains carried iron ore to be smelted on an 80km/50-mile circular line. The locomotives were based on a Swiss design. They had a sloping front so that the driver could see easily from the cab.

GOING UNDERGROUND

RAILWAY NETWORKS made it easier for people to travel from the country to cities and towns to shop or work. During the 1800s, the streets within cities became extremely crowded with people and traffic. One way of coping with the problem of moving around the cities was to tunnel underground.

The world's first underground passenger railway, or subway system, opened in 1863. It was the Metropolitan Line between Paddington Station and Farringdon Street in London, England. Steam locomotives hauled the passenger carriages, and smoke in the tunnels was a big problem. The locomotives were fitted with structures called condensers that were supposed to absorb the smoke, but they did not work properly. Passengers on the trains passed through a fog-like darkness. Those waiting at the stations choked on the smoke drifting out from the tunnels.

Electric trains were the answer. The first underground electric railway opened in London in 1890. Today, nearly every major city in the world has such a system.

Cut-and-cover construction
The first underground passenger railways were built using a new method called cut-and-cover construction. A large trench – usually 10m/33ft wide by 5m/16ft deep – was cut into the earth along the proposed route. Then the trench was lined with brickwork and it was roofed over. After that, the streets were re-laid on top of the tunnel.

Tunnel maze
This cross-section of the underground system in Central London in 1864 shows the proposed route of the new Charing Cross Line beneath the existing Metropolitan Line. Deep-level underground railways were not built until 1890, when developments such as ways of digging deeper tunnels, electric locomotives, better lifts and escalators became a reality.

Underground shelters
Londoners came up with another use for their city's warren of underground railway tunnels during World War II (1939–45). They used them as deep shelters from night-time bombing raids. The electric lines were switched off, and people slept wherever they could find enough room to lie down. Canteens were set up on many platforms. More than half a million litres/130,000 gallons of tea and cocoa were served every night.

Moving with the times

Washington DC Metro opened in 1976 in the USA, and was at that time one of the world's most up-to-date subway system. The automatic trains had no drivers. However, several accidents and problems, especially when nine people died in 2009, led to drivers being put back in the cabs. Passengers using the air-conditioned carriages have a smooth, fast ride owing to the latest techniques in train and track construction. The airy, 183m/600ft-long stations are much more spacious than those built during the early 1900s.

FACT BOX

• The world's busiest underground system is in Seoul, South Korea, with over 2,500 million trips made yearly.

• The New York City Subway in the USA has the most stations, with 468.

• The world's second electric underground railway was the 4km/2½-mile long line in Budapest, Hungary in 1896.

Mechanical earthworm

The cutting head of a Tunnel-Boring Machine (TBM), which was used to bore the Channel Tunnel between England and France. The 8m/26ft-wide cutting head is covered with diamond-studded teeth. As the TBM rotates, the teeth rip through the earth. The waste material, or spoil, falls on to a conveyor belt and is transported to the surface. The cutting head grips against the sides of the tunnel and inches farther forward under the pressure of huge rams. As the tunnel is cut, cranes line the tunnel with curved concrete segments that arrive on conveyors at the top and bottom of the TBM.

Overground undergrounds

Work started on the first 10km/6-mile long section of the Paris *Metro* in 1898 and took over two years to complete. The engineers who designed early underground railway systems, such as the Paris *Metro,* often found it quicker and easier to take sections above ground, particularly when crossing rivers. The station entrances were designed by French architect Hector Guimard in the then-fashionable Art Nouveau style. They made the Paris *Metro* one of the most distinctive and stylish underground systems in the world.

RIDING HIGH

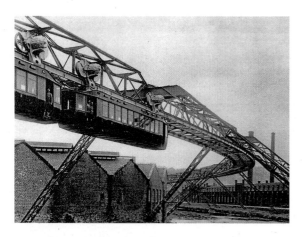

I N SOME OF the world's cities, the solution to overcrowded streets was to build rail networks above ground level. The earliest kind of overhead trains ran on a twin-rail track. The track was raised above the ground on arching, viaduct-like supports. These 'elevated railways' were built in several American and European cities from the mid-1800s.

Today, some overhead trains run along a single rail called a monorail. Some are suspended systems in which the train hangs beneath the rail. Others are straddle systems in which the train sits over the rail.

Twin-rail systems called Light Rapid Transit (LRT) are now more common than monorails. They are described as 'light' because they carry fewer people and therefore need lighter-weight vehicles and track than mainline, or 'heavy', railways. In many cities, LRT railcars are like a cross between a tram or streetcar and a train. They run on rails through streets, as well as through underground tunnels and along elevated tracks.

Wonder of Wuppertal
The oldest working monorail in the world is located in Wuppertal, Germany. Almost 20 million passengers have traversed the 13.3km/8-mile route since it opened in 1901. It is suspended 10m/33ft above the ground. The wheels run along the top of the rail.

Flying train
Inventor George Bennie's experimental monorail was one of the strangest ever built. The streamlined machine was named the Railplane. It had aircraft propellers front and back to thrust it along. It first 'flew' in July 1930, along a 40m/130ft-long test track near Glasgow, Scotland.

Climb every mountain
The Paris funicular climbs to the city's highest point, the top of Montmartre. Funiculars were invented during the 1800s and are used to move carriages up and down hillsides or steep slopes. Usually, there are two parallel tracks. Each one has a passenger-carrying car attached. In the early days, each car carried a large water tank that was filled with water at the top of the slope and emptied at the bottom. The extra weight of the car going down pulled the lighter car up. Later funiculars have winding drums powered by electricity to haul a cable up and down.

Tomorrow's world

During the 1950s, American film producer Walt Disney wanted to have a monorail for his futuristic Tomorrowland attraction when he built his first Disneyland theme park in California. The monorail opened in 1959 and was an immediate success with visitors. Disney was trying to promote monorails as the transport system of the future, but his railroad had just the opposite effect. For many years, monorails were seen as little more than amusement-park rides.

FACT BOX
- New Yorkers nicknamed their elevated railroad the 'El'. It opened in 1868. By 1900, more than 300 locomotives and 1,000 passenger carriages were operating on its 58km/36-mile long network.

Not everyone's darling

The monorail system in Sydney, Australia, links the heart of the city to a tourist development in nearby Darling Harbour. It has proved to be popular since it opened in 1988, carrying about 30,000 people a day along its 3.5km/2-mile long route. Many people who lived in Sydney were concerned that the elevated route would be an eyesore, particularly in older parts of the city. Protesters tried hard to block the monorail's construction. In 2013 it closed to make way for extending the traditional light rail system.

London's LRT

The Docklands Light Railway in London opened in 1987. It was Britain's first Light Rapid Transit (LRT) to have driverless vehicles controlled by a computerized control system. However, it was not Britain's first LRT. That prize went to Newcastle's Tyne and Wear Metro, which began running in 1980. LRTs provide a frequent service, with unstaffed stations and automatic ticket machines. Many cities throughout the world have chosen to install them in preference to monorails because they are cheaper to run.

MONORAIL

Monorails date back to the 1820s. As with early trains, these early monorails were pulled by horses and carried heavy materials such as building bricks, rather than passengers. About 60 years later, engineers designed steam locomotives that hauled carriages along A-shaped frameworks. However, neither the trains nor the carriages were very stable. Loads had to be carefully balanced on either side of the A-frame to stop them tipping off.

Today's monorails are completely stable, with several sets of rubber wheels to give a smooth ride. They are powered by electricity, and many are driverless. Like fully automatic LRTs, driverless monorail trains are controlled by computers that tell them when to stop, start, speed up or slow down.

Monorails are not widely used today because they are more expensive to run than two-track railways. The special monorail track costs more to build, is more of an eyesore than two-track lines and the cars cannot be switched from one track to another.

Staying on track
Vertical sets of running wheels carry the weight of this modern monorail and keep it on top of the huge rail. Other horizontal sets of wheels, called guides and stabilizers, run along the sides of the rail. They keep the train on course and stop it from tipping when it goes around bends.

MODEL MONORAIL

You will need: sheet of protective paper, 72cm/28¼in length of wood (4cm/1½in wide and 4cm/1½in deep), acrylic paints, paintbrush, water pot, 67cm/26½in length of plastic curtain rail (with screws, end fittings and four plastic runners), saw, screwdriver, sheet of red card stock, pencil, ruler, scissors, double-sided sticky tape, 18cm/7in length of 2.5cm/1in thick foam board, glue and glue brush, black felt-tip pen.

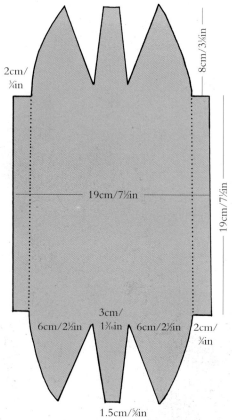

2cm/¾in
8cm/3⅛in
19cm/7½in
19cm/7½in
3cm/1³⁄₁₆in
6cm/2½in 6cm/2½in 2cm/¾in
1.5cm/⅝in

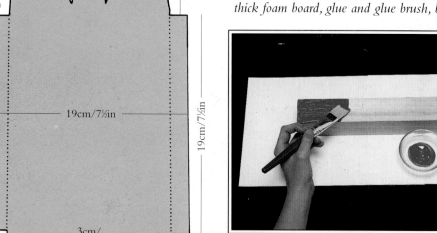

1 Cover the work surface with paper to protect it. Then paint the block of wood yellow. Let the first coat dry thoroughly before applying a second coat of paint.

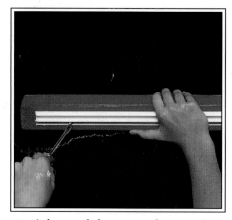

2 Ask an adult to saw the curtain rail to size if necessary. Place the track centrally on the wood and screw it into place. Screw in the end fittings at one end of the rail.

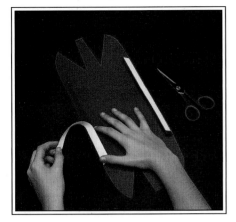

3 Copy the template on to the red card and cut it out. Score along the dotted lines and fold inwards. Stick double-sided tape along the outside of each folded section.

4 Remove the backing from the tape. Stick one side of the foam on to it. Fold the card over and press the other piece of double-sided tape to the opposite side of the foam.

5 Overlap the pointed ends at the back and front of the train and glue. Then glue the inside end of the top flaps, back and front. Fold them over and press firmly to secure.

6 Pencil in windows along both sides of the train. Fill them in with a black felt-tip pen. Paint decorative black and yellow stripes along the bottom of the windows.

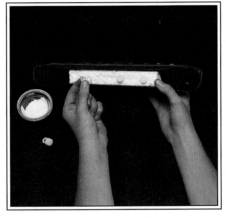

7 Put a dab of glue on the 'eye' end of each plastic runner. Hold the train, foam bottom towards you. Push each runner in turn into the foam at roughly equal intervals.

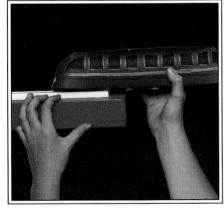

8 Stand the track on a flat surface. At the end of the track without an end stop, feed each plastic runner into the track. Run the train back and forth along the track.

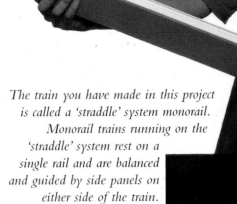

The train you have made in this project is called a 'straddle' system monorail. Monorail trains running on the 'straddle' system rest on a single rail and are balanced and guided by side panels on either side of the train.

WORKING ON THE RAILROAD

A S THE RAILWAYS grew ever larger, so did the number of people employed to keep them running safely and on time. In Britain, for example, about 47,000 people worked for the railway companies by the late 1840s. Today, about 100,000 people are employed on the British railways – seven times less than during World War I (1914–18). One reason is that some jobs that were once done by people, such as selling tickets, are now done by machines. Automation has not been widespread, however. Most railways have little money to buy computers and control systems.

Station-masters and train conductors are just some of the people who talk to passengers and deal with their needs. Most railway employees work behind the scenes, however, and rarely meet passengers. Managers plan how many trains should run on a particular line, how often and how fast. Engineering teams check and keep the tracks, signals and other equipment in safe working order.

Standing on the footplate
Two men worked in the cab. They stood on the footplate because there were no seats. The driver was in charge. He managed the engine controls and the main brakes and kept a sharp look out for signals and anything blocking the track. The fireman stoked the fire and checked the boiler.

Laying track
Track workers check a section of track that has been newly laid with stone ballast, sleepers (ties) and rail. Rails should be checked regularly for cracks and deterioration. The ground beneath the rail can also subside and twist the rails.

Building trains
Workers in a factory are assembling an aluminium-bodied diesel train. Modern trains are built of either steel or aluminium sections welded together into a strong single unit. Separate units, such as the driver's cab, air-conditioning engine and toilets are added to the car later.

In the driving seat

Compared to the older steam engines, life is fairly comfortable in the cabs of modern locomotives. For a start, the driver can sit down. They are also protected from the weather inside fully enclosed cabs, and they do not have to stick their heads outside to see the track ahead. Today's drivers still manage the controls and brakes, and watch out for signals and obstacles on the track. They also have a lot of help from computerized systems.

Bug bath

The front of this train is being cleaned by hand, since this is the most effective way to remove the accumulation of flying insects on the cab windows. The bodies of most trains are cleaned in automatic washing plants using revolving brushes, high-pressure water jets and powerful cleaning agents that meet high environmental standards. In most cases, trains are cleaned every 24 hours when they come back to their home depot for examination and routine servicing.

Chefs on board

Armies of chefs and kitchen staff play an important role in making sure passengers do not go hungry during the journey. Most cooked food is prepared on board using microwave ovens and electric stovetops. Most long-distance trains have dining and buffet cars, where passengers can take refreshment during their journeys. Even smaller trains often have buffet cars or mobile buffet trolleys.

DRESSED FOR THE JOB

Many different railway workers began wearing special hats and uniforms during the 1840s, from train drivers to station-masters. A uniform makes the wearer look smart and efficient and lets him or her stand out in a crowd. This is essential if a passenger is looking for help in a busy station. Uniforms are issued by the railway companies. Each company usually has its own design for hat badges and uniform buttons.

In the past, different kinds of hat or badge often went with different jobs. The drivers of steam locomotives, for example, used to wear caps with shiny tops. Firemen were not issued with hats or uniforms. They wore overalls and often covered their heads with a knotted handkerchief. The first station-masters wore top hats instead of caps to show how important they were. When they later switched to caps, the brim was often decorated with gold braid, similar to the one you can make in this project.

Dressed for the job
A station-master and guard at Osaka Railway Station in Japan wear their distinctive dark uniforms, caps and sashes. The station-master, or area manager, has an extremely important role in running the railways. He or she is in charge of running the station and must make sure that trains arrive and depart on time.

STATION-MASTER'S CAP

You will need: thin red card stock measuring 60x9cm/24x3½in, masking tape, thin red card stock measuring 11x11cm/4¼x4¼in, pencil, scissors, thin red card stock measuring 26x15cm/10¼x6in, glue and glue brush, sheet of white paper, pair of compasses, black felt, black paint, paintbrush, water pot, 40cm/16in gold braid, card stock, gold paint.

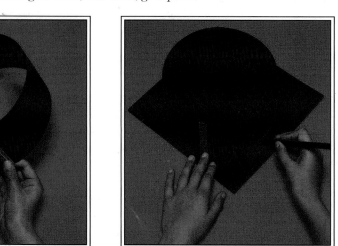

1 Wrap the 60x9cm/24x3½in piece of red card around your head to get the right size. Then stick the two ends together with masking tape to make the circular crown of the hat.

2 Place the crown on the 11x11cm/4½x4½in piece of red card. Hold the crown firmly and draw around it. Cut out the circle to make the top of your hat.

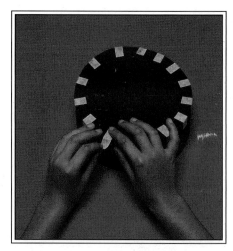

3 Place the card circle on top of the crown of the hat. Join the two parts of the hat together using lots of strips of masking tape all the way around the join.

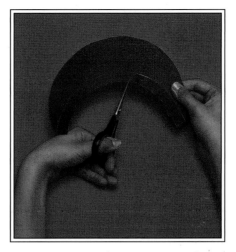

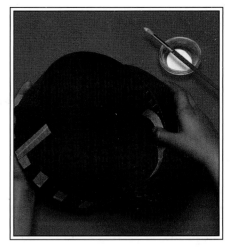

4 Place the hat over part of the 26x15cm/10¼x6in piece of card. Draw a semi-circle by tracing around the hat edge. Start from one end of the semicircle, and draw a crescent.

5 Use a pair of compasses to draw another semicircle 2cm/¾in in from the first. Cut out the crescent. Make cuts into the inner semicircle band all the way around to make tabs.

6 Fold the tabs up and glue around the edge of the crown where the peak will go. Fit the tabs inside the crown and stick them down. Cover the tabs with tape to hold firm.

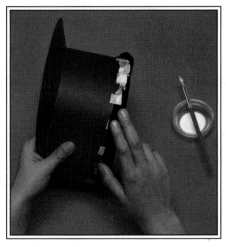

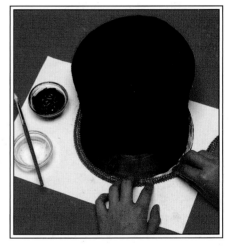

7 Place the hat, top down, on to a sheet of paper. Draw and cut out a circle 1cm/½in wider than the hat. Pin it on the felt and cut out a felt circle. Glue on to the top of the hat.

8 Cut a 60x10cm/24x4in piece of felt. Glue this to the side of the hat, folding under at the bottom. At the peak, make a 2cm/¾in cut in the felt, and trim off the excess.

9 Give the peak two coats of black paint. Let the paint dry between coats. Then glue on a piece of gold braid as shown.

10 Design your own hat badge or copy the one shown in the picture. Draw it on a small piece of card and paint it gold. When the paint is dry, cut it out. Glue it to the front of the hat.

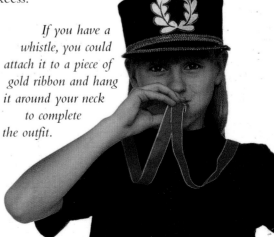

If you have a whistle, you could attach it to a piece of gold ribbon and hang it around your neck to complete the outfit.

RIDING IN STYLE

First-class comforts
By the late 1800s, first-class passengers such as these elegantly dressed ladies enjoyed every comfort on their journey. There were soft, padded benches and armchairs and cloth-covered tea tables. The design of luxury railway carriages was based on that of top-class hotels. Windows had thick, plush curtains and fittings were made of polished wood and brass.

I T WAS SOME time before riding aboard a passenger train was as comfortable as waiting in one of the splendid stations. Before the 1850s, there were few luxuries and no toilets, even on long journeys. The overall comfort of the journey depended on how much money you had paid for your ticket. First-class carriages were – and still are – the most expensive and the most comfortable way to travel. Then came second class, third class and sometimes even fourth class.

The pioneer of comfortable rail travel was an American businessman called George Pullman. In 1859, after a particularly unpleasant train journey, he designed a carriage in which "people could sleep and eat with more ease and comfort". Pullman launched his sleeping car in 1864, and was soon exporting luxury sleeping and dining carriages around the world.

Royal seal of approval
This luxurious railway carriage was made for Britain's Queen Victoria, who reigned from 1837 until her death in 1901. It had padded walls, thick carpets, expensive paintings on the walls and the finest decoration. Many European kings and queens had their own carriages built so that they could travel in royal style. Queen Victoria's carriage included a sleeping car, and it is thought she enjoyed sleeping in it more than at her palaces.

The Blue Train
South Africa's Blue Trains run between Cape Town and Pretoria in South Africa and are regarded as the most luxurious trains in the world. Passengers benefit from a 24-hour butler and laundry service and two lounge cars, and all the suites are equipped with televisions and telephones.

Lap of luxury

The *Orient Express* first graced the railways of Europe in 1883. It formed a scheduled link between Paris, France, and Bucharest in Romania. The scheduled service stopped running in May 1977, and was replaced by a new 'tourist-only' *Orient Express* in May 1982. Passengers can once again enjoy the comfortable sleeping cars with velvet curtains, plush seats and five-course French cuisine in a Pullman dining car.

A rocky ride

The Canadian has a domed glass roof so that it offers spectacular views during the 4,467km/ 2,776-mile journey from Toronto, near the east coast of Canada, to Vancouver, on the west. The journey lasts for three days and takes in the rolling prairies of Saskatchewan, Edmonton and Alberta. It then begins the gradual ascent through the foothills of the Rocky Mountains.

Lounging about

Long-distance trains on the Indian Pacific line from Sydney, on the Pacific Ocean, to Perth, on the Indian Ocean, are well equipped for the 65-hour journey across Australia. Indeed, they are described as being "luxury hotels on wheels". Passengers can relax and enjoy the entertainment provided in the comfortable surroundings of the train's lounge cars. These trains also have cafeterias, smart dining cars, club cars and two classes of accommodation. Passengers can eat, drink and sleep in comfort. The trains are even equipped with a honeymoon suite and a sick bay.

ADVERTISING

I N THE EARLY DAYS of the rail, radio and television had not been invented. Rail companies had to rely on printed advertisements to attract potential customers. Posters have long been used to entice train passengers. At first, they were little more than printed handbills – a few words with the odd black-and-white picture. "The Wonder of 1851! From York to London and back for a Crown", read one British rail-company poster. A crown was 5 shillings (the equivalent of 25p/38¢).

Early posters were so basic because machines for printing words and pictures in colour were not developed until the late 1800s. Posters soon became more elaborate. For example, French railways used eye-catching posters to advertise their new electric services in the early 1900s. The pictures on early railway posters usually showed the destination rather than the train – people travel on trains because they want to go somewhere. By promoting new services and encouraging people to take the train, rail companies helped to improve advertising methods.

Atlantic crossing
Britain's Southern Railway promoted both its own train services and those of shipping company White Star in this poster from the late 1920s. Passengers could take the train to Southampton in England and then join a White Star ship for the crossing to New York in the USA. At that time, many railways owned shipping lines or worked with steamship companies.

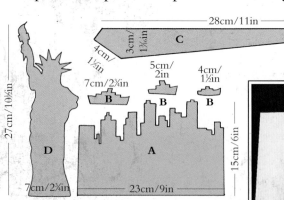

MAKE A POSTER

You will need: *protective paper, 27x23cm/ 10½x9in dark blue card stock, acrylic paints, paintbrush, water pot, glue and glue brush, 37.5x25cm/14¾x10in ream card stock, 23x8cm/9x3⅛in and 30x5cm/12x2in light blue card stock, pencil, ruler, scissors, large sheet of black card stock, 23x5.5cm/ 9x2¼in blue card stock, 30x10cm/12x4in yellow card stock, black pen.*

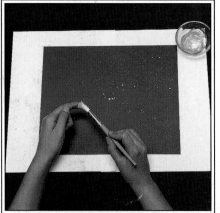

1 Cover the work surface and lay the dark blue card on to it. Mix some yellow and white paint, load a paintbrush with paint and then flick spots on to the card as shown above.

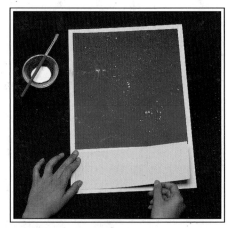

2 Glue it on to the cream card, leaving a 1cm/⅜in border at top and sides and 9.5cm/3¾in at the bottom. Glue the 23x8cm/9x3⅛in light blue card at the bottom.

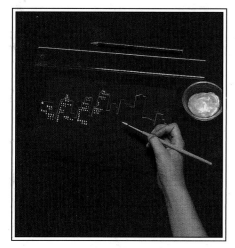

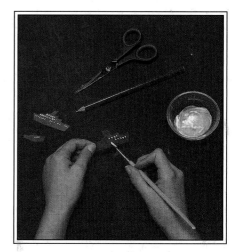

3 Copy the New York skyline template (A) using the black card. Use the yellow-and-white paint mixture to make spots for lights in the windows. Cut the skyline out.

4 When the paint is completely dry, glue the back of the skyline template. Line up the bottom edge with the top edge of the light blue card and then press down firmly.

5 Copy and cut out the ship templates (B) using the black card. Use the yellow-and-white paint mixture to paint portholes on the ships. Leave the paint to dry.

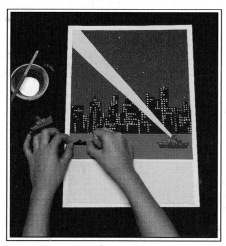

7 Copy the statue template (D) or enlarge it on a photocopier and trace it on to yellow card. Add details with black felt tip pen. Cut out the statue and glue it in position.

6 Glue the blue card on to the bottom of the skyline. Then glue on the ships. Copy and cut out the spotlight template (C) using the 30x5cm/12x2in light blue card and glue on the largest ship as shown.

Now that you know how to make a poster, you can design your own. Collect photographs and cuttings from magazines and tourist information leaflets of a town or a famous tourist attraction nearby. Photocopy them to the size you want and then trace them on to card in the same way you have done for this project.

TRAINS ON FILM

WHEN THE French brothers Auguste and Louis Lumière showed one of their short films in 1895 of a train pulling into a station, many of the audience fled. They were terrified that the train would burst out of the screen into the room. Hardly anyone had ever seen a moving picture before, and people found them frighteningly realistic.

Trains have had a starring role in the movies ever since. The climax of many early films, for example, involved the 'baddies' tying the heroine to a train track, while the hero rushed to save her. Film-makers have continued to use trains to keep audiences on the edge of their seats. Nearly all the best train movies have been adventure thrillers.

In the early days, filming moving trains was a risky business. The cameras were bolted on the locomotive, while the camera operator leaned out or rode on a train on a parallel track. Such risks would not be taken today.

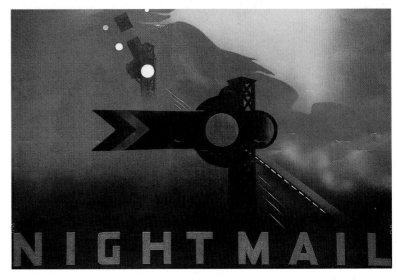

Poetry, please
Night Mail (1936) showed scenes of mail being dropped off, and collected, by the 'Night Mail' train in Scotland. It was made to show postal workers how letters were carried on the mail train between England and Scotland. Later, the British-born American poet W. H. Auden was asked to write verse for a voice-over. His poetry echoes the noises of the train as it made its long journey through the night.

Tears on the train
In the 1945 film *Brief Encounter*, two people find romance in a railway station. Their love is doomed, however, as both are married. Much of the action was shot at Carnforth Station in England.

Railway children to the rescue
When a landslide threatens to derail a steam train in *The Railway Children* (1970), the children save the day by turning red petticoats into warning flags to signal to the driver. The film used engines and carriages on a heritage railway in West Yorkshire, England. It gives an insight into how steam trains and stations operated in the early 1900s.

Smashing finish

A runaway train crashes through the walls of the station concourse in the thrilling climax to the 1976 action movie *Silver Streak*. Almost the whole movie is set on the train, during its two-and-a-half-day journey from Los Angeles to Chicago. Gene Wilder stars as the passenger who witnesses a murder on his first night and spends the rest of the journey battling off the baddies.

Bond on board

Daniel Craig plays the tough British agent in the 23rd James Bond movie, *Skyfall* (released in 2012). Like all Bond movies, it is packed with breathtaking stunts and chases. In the opening scene, James Bond faces a gripping fight on top of a speeding train. The sequence was filmed on top of a real moving train and Craig did not use a stunt double. Stunt men were used for other dangerous scenes.

Animal action

Indiana Jones and the Last Crusade (released in 1989) opens with an exciting flashback. Young Indie is trying to escape pursuers by clambering along the top of a steam train. Chases are the stock-in-trade of adventure movies, but this one is different. The steam locomotive is hauling circus wagons. Indie falls into various cages, where he finds snakes, a rhinoceros and even a lion.

Race to the death

A speeding freight train carrying a stolen nuclear weapon is the setting for the nail-biting closing sequence of the 1996 action movie *Broken Arrow*. The hero (shown left, played by Christian Slater) scrambles over and under the freight wagons, as he attempts to wrest control of the train back from the villain (played by John Travolta) and disarm the bomb before it explodes.

RECORD BREAKERS

BIGGEST, FASTEST, steepest – trains and railways have been setting records ever since they were invented. Official speed records began when George and Robert Stephenson's *Rocket* reached a top speed of 48.3kmh/30mph in the 1829 Rainhill Trials. By the end of the 1800s, engineers were competing to produce a steam engine that could break the 100mph (161kmh) record.

Time-keeping was inaccurate until speedometers were fitted to locomotives during the 1900s. An American *No. 999* locomotive may have briefly managed 161kmh/100mph in 1893. Steam trains capable of sustaining this kind of speed over long distances did not enter service until the 1930s.

World records are usually set over short distances, by locomotives hauling fewer carriages. When, for example, the 200mph (321.9kmh) barrier was broken in 1955 by two French Railways electric locomotives, each one was pulling just three carriages.

Claim to fame

The New York Central & Hudson River Railroad (NYC & HRR) built the 4-4-0 *No. 999* to haul its Empire State Express. On 11 May 1893, it was claimed that *No. 999* recorded a run of 181kmh/112mph between New York and Buffalo. The V-shaped 'cowcatcher' at the front was one of the distinctive features of American locomotives. Since great lengths of the American railroads were not fenced off, it was essential to protect the front of the locomotives from wandering animals such as buffalo. The cowcatcher performed this function very well.

Champion of steam

On 3 July 1938, Britain's A4-class Pacific *Mallard*'s sleek, streamlined bodywork helped it to set the world speed record for a steam locomotive. With driver Joe Duddington at the controls, backed up by fireman Tommy Bray, it reached 201kmh/125mph – a world steam record that remains unbeaten today. *Mallard* was designed by British engineer Sir Nigel Gresley. It remained in everyday service until the early 1960s.

• The world's fastest regular passenger trains can exceed 300kmh/185mph. They include France's TGV (*Train à Grande Vitesse*) POS, ICE (*InterCity Express*) 3 trains in Germany, E5 Series 'bullet trains' of Japan, Siemens AVE trains between Madrid and Barcelona in Spain, and Class 373 Eurostar services between London and Paris.

• The longest and heaviest freight train on record ran in West Virginia in 1967. The 500 coal wagons weighed 42,000 tons and stretched a distance of 6.5km/4 miles.

• With a route length of 57km/35½ miles, the Gotthard Base Tunnel (GBT) that runs through the Swiss Alps is the longest and deepest traffic tunnel in the world.

Steep slopes

The *Pilatusbahn* in Lucerne, Switzerland, is the steepest rack-and-pinion, or cog, railway in the world, climbing to a height of 2,073m/6,801ft above sea level. This system uses a rack laid between the rails. This links with a cog wheel under the engine as it drives the train up the steep 1:2 gradients (1m up for every 2m along).

Overcoming the obstacles

Mount Washington Railway in New Hampshire in the USA became the world's first mountain rack-and-pinion railway when it opened in 1869. At this time, mountain climbing and sightseeing by steam railway was a great tourist attraction.

Shapes and sizes

1. Scotsman Patrick Stirling's Single locomotives, dating from 1870, are particularly striking locomotives. The driving wheels of these steam engines were a massive 2.5m/8ft in diameter.
2. In 2007, a specially modified French TGV (*Train à Grande Vitesse*), equipped with larger wheels, set a record of 574.8kmh/357mph.
3. By winning the Rainhill Trials in 1829, Robert and George Stephenson's *Rocket* put steam travel firmly on the world map, making this one of the most famous steam locomotives in the world.
4. The world's largest and most powerful steam engines are without doubt the Union Pacific Big Boys, each weighing over 500 tons.

1 — 16m/52½ft — — 4.1m/13½ft

2 — 22m/72ft — — 4.2m/13¾ft — 5m/16ft

3 — 7.3m/24ft — — 4.9m/16ft

4 — 40.4m/132½ft —

HIGH-SPEED TRAINS

THE RECORD-HOLDERS of today are the high-speed electric trains that whisk passengers between major cities at 250–300kmh/155–185mph. These high-speed trains are the railway's answer to the competition from aircraft and motorways that grew up after World War II (1939–45). High-speed trains can travel at well over the legal limits for road traffic. Although they cannot travel as fast as planes, they save passengers time by taking them into the middle of cities. In some cases, high-speed trains even beat the flying time between major cities, such as London and Paris.

The world's first high-speed intercity passenger service was launched in Japan on 1 October 1964. It linked the capital, Tokyo, with the major industrial city of Osaka in the south. The average speed of these trains – 220kmh/137mph – broke all the records for a passenger train service. The service was officially named the *Tokaido Shinkansen* (new high-speed railway), but its trains soon became known as Bullet Trains – because of their speed and the bullet-shaped noses of the locomotives.

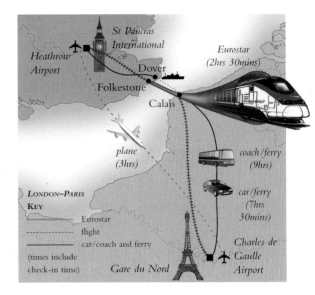

Market leader
The Eurostar has become the quickest way to travel between the capital cities London, England, and Paris, France. It cuts out time-consuming airport check-in and transfer periods. Ferry crossings dramatically increase the journey times by car, coach or bus.

Rocket on rails
JR500 trains on Japan's *Tokaido Shinkansen* and *Sanyo Shinkansen* lines are as streamlined as a jetplane. Introduced in 1997, they reach 300kmh/185mph.

Stacking the odds

On some high-speed trains, such as this French TGV, passengers ride in double-decker carriages. The initials TGV are short for *Train à Grande Vitesse* (high-speed train). The operational speed of these French trains is 300kmh/185mph. TGVs also hold the current world speed record for a conventional wheeled manned train.

Melting the ICE

Germany's ICE (InterCity Express) high-speed trains reached speeds of more than 400kmh/250mph during tests, before they entered service in 1992. Their maximum operational speed is 320kmh/200mph. Like other high-speed trains, they are streamlined to reduce the slowing effects of drag.

Swedish tilter

The Swedish X2000 tilting electric trains have an average speed of 155kmh/95mph and a top speed of 204kmh/127mph. Tilting trains lean into curves to allow them to travel around bends at faster speeds than non-tilting trains.

Spanish speeder

Spain's elegant high-speed trains are called AVEs (*Alta Velocidad España,* or high speed of Spain). Some average operational speeds exceed 300kmh/185mph. They entered service on Spain's first high-speed railway, between Madrid and Seville, in 1992. Like all high-speed trains, AVEs take their power from overhead electricity lines.

INVESTING IN THE FUTURE

To accelerate to speeds of up to 320kmh/200mph, or even beyond, trains need to run on specially constructed tracks, with as few curves and slopes as possible. The tracks have to be wider apart than was usual in the past. A speeding train stirs the wind into eddies, which can buffet a passing train and jolt its passengers. The ride is also smoother and faster if continuously welded rails are used. If they have their own, dedicated lines, high-speed trains do not have to fit in with the timetables of ordinary, less speedy trains that would slow them down.

Throughout the world, rail companies are investing huge sums of money in building new lines or upgrading old track to carry their high-speed trains. In a few countries, people believe the future of land travel lies with an entirely different kind of train. For example, maglev trains 'fly' just above their track, raised and propelled by magnetism.

Star performer
The Eurostar trains operate between England and Continental Europe. They can accelerate to 300kmh/185mph – and even greater speeds where the tracks allow. For safety reasons, they pass through the Channel Tunnel at a reduced speed of 160kmh/100mph, taking just 35 minutes to travel between the coastal ports of Calais and Folkestone. In 2007, the English section of track, HS1 (High Speed 1), or the Channel Tunnel Rail Link (CTRL), opened direct into St Pancras Station in London.

More trains, please
Rail links need to expand if they are to cope with the booming global population. Around 60 per cent of the world's population is expected to live and work in cities by the year 2030, and those people will need to get around. Fortunately, more trains are on their way. In the USA, for instance, train lines are being built or expanded in cities that were not previously thought of as major transportation hubs, such as Denver, Los Angeles, Miami, Phoenix and Salt Lake City. Houston, one of America's fastest-growing cities, opened its METRORail light rail Red Line (shown above) in 2004, before adding Green and Purple Lines in 2015.

It's on the cards
Many metro systems provide commuters with the option to buy a plastic card (like a credit or debit card) that is digitally loaded with a prepaid fare. The passenger can then get through the ticket gates by tapping the card on an electronic reader, or by waving the card close to the reader. The earliest example of such smartcards was Hong Kong's Octopus card, introduced in 1997. It was followed by Japan's Suica (Super Urban Intelligent CArd), London's Oyster and South Korea's T-Money.

What, no driver?

There are already trains that can operate entirely independently of human control, though only a few passenger railways in the world currently use them. Examples can be found in Vancouver, Canada, and in Denmark's capital Copenhagen. Many other lines have semi-autonomous trains that can navigate themselves but still have a human onboard to start the train or open and close the doors. There are plans for Honolulu, Hawaii, to introduce the USA's first fully autonomous rail system, based upon the one used in Copenhagen. Meanwhile, London hopes to launch its 'New Tube' between 2025 and 2033. This will be a wave of 250 fully autonomous trains added to the London Underground. Self-driving trains allow a more frequent service with more consistent intervals at busy times, as demonstrated by Vancouver's SkyTrain (shown here), which runs on a network of underground and elevated guideways.

High-speed magnetism

Japanese maglev (short for magnetic levitation) trains have reached the astonishing speed of 603kmh/ 374½mph on the specially constructed Yamanashi test line. This outstrips the world's fastest wheeled train, the TGV, by 28.2kmh/17½mph. Maglevs are so fast because they float above their track. They do not have wheels and they do not touch the rails. Rails solved the problem of the slowing force of friction between wheels and roads. Maglevs are the answer to reducing friction between wheels and rails. At present, only three countries – China, Japan and South Korea – have commercial maglev systems, but there are plans to introduce them elsewhere.

In the loop

The Shanghai Maglev Train, also known as the Transrapid, is the fastest commercial train currently in operation, with a top speed of 430kmh/270mph. However, at higher speeds air turbulence can affect passenger comfort, causing a feeling of motion sickness. The solution may be the use of enclosed tubes that reduce air resistance. Such as idea is being put forward by American entrepreneur Elon Musk, whose Hyperloop promises speeds up to an incredible 1,220kmh/760mph. The inventor's futuristic concept involves linking big cities via a network of trains that would travel inside reduced-pressure tubes. Designs for test tracks and capsules are being developed, and construction of a full-scale prototype is underway.

FLOATING TRAINS

MAGLEV (MAGNETICALLY levitated) trains need their own specially constructed tracks, called guideways, to move along. The trains are raised and pushed along by powerful electromagnets. The special thing about magnets is that 'unlike' ends or poles (north and south) attract each other or pull together, while 'like' poles (north and north, or south and south) repel or push apart. To make an electromagnet, an electric current flows through a wire or other conductor. When the direction of the current is changed, the magnetic poles switch, too.

A maglev train rises when one set of electromagnets beneath it repels another set in the guideway. The maglev is moved by other electromagnets changing magnetic fields (switching poles). A set of electromagnets in the guideway ahead attracts electromagnets beneath the train, pulling it forward. As the train passes, the electromagnetic fields are switched. The maglev is repelled and pushed onwards to the next set of magnets on the guideway.

The main advantage of maglevs over normal wheeled trains is that they are faster because they are not slowed by friction. Maglevs are also quieter and use less energy than wheeled trains.

Maglevs get moving
The technology behind maglevs was developed in the 1960s. The world's first service opened at Birmingham City Airport in Britain in the mid–1980s. Japan and Germany now lead the field in developing the technology.

MODEL MAGLEV

You will need: *yellow card stock, pencil, ruler, scissors, red card stock, green card stock, glue and glue brush, blue card stock, double-sided sticky tape, 30x10cm/12x4in wooden board, bradawl, two 8cm/3⅛in lengths thin dowel, wood glue, green and red paint, paintbrush, water pot, four magnets with holes in their middles.*

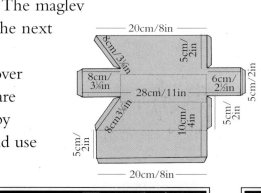

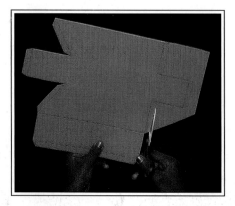

1 Copy the template on to a thin piece of yellow card. The tabs around the side of the template should be 1cm/½in wide. Carefully cut around the outline.

2 Cut two strips of red card and glue them to each side of the template as shown. Cut the green card into window shapes and glue them to the front and sides.

3 Continue to glue the windows to each side of the train to make two even rows. Cut two small blue card circles for headlights. Glue them to the front of the train as shown.

4 Leave the train template until the glue is completely dry. Then carefully use a pair of scissors and a ruler to score along the dotted lines for the tabs and the folds of the train.

5 Bend along the scored lines to form the basic shape of the train as shown above. Then cut small strips of double-sided sticky tape and stick them along each tab.

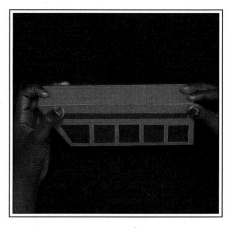

6 Stick the front and back sections of the train to the tabs on one side of the train. Repeat for the other side. Then stick the base section of the train to the opposite side.

7 Use a bradawl to pierce two holes in the wooden base, 9cm/3½in in from each end. Enlarge with a pencil. Put wood glue on the end of each dowel and push one into each hole.

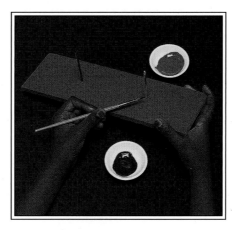

8 When the glue is dry give the base a coat of green paint. Paint two coats, letting the first dry before you apply the second. Then paint the dowel uprights a bright red.

9 Press the two magnets together so that they repel. These sides are the same poles – north or south. Use double-sided tape to fix the magnets to the base with like poles facing up.

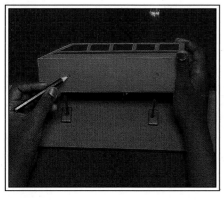

10 Hold the base of the train up to the dowel uprights. Mark two points in the centre of the base the same distance as between the uprights. Pierce through the marks.

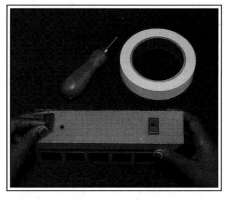

11 Push magnets over the dowel uprights to repel those on the base. Take them off and tape them over the holes in the train base so that these like poles face upwards.

Push the train over the dowel uprights. Like poles on the wooden base and the train base face each other, making the train 'float' in mid-air. You can feel the magnetic force if you push down on the train.

GLOSSARY

Alta Velocidad Espanã (AVE)
The name of the high-speed passenger trains that operate in Spain.

Automatic Train Protection (ATP)
An advanced safety feature operating on some trains running only on British railway networks. Trains pick up electronic signals from the track, which tell the driver to slow or stop the train. ATP also automatically slows the train if the driver exceeds the speed limit.

Automatic Warning System (AWS)
A safety feature of all trains running only on British railway networks. AWS informs the driver whether the track ahead is clear. Electric magnets between the rails send a message to the train, causing a bell to sound in the driver's cab if the track is clear. Otherwise, the magnet stays 'dead' and a horn sounds. AWS operates the brakes automatically if the driver does not respond to the signals.

bogie
Also known as a truck, this is a unit placed underneath a locomotive that guides the train around curves in the track. The bogie also provides extra support for the locomotive. Four or six pivoted wheels are mounted on one bogie.

boiler
The part of a steam engine where steam is produced through the action of heat on water in the boiler tubes.

brake van
A vehicle at the back of trains, also known as a caboose. A guard riding in the brake van applied brakes in the van on instruction from the driver in the locomotive at the front. This ensured that all the carriages of the train stayed coupled.

buffer
Rigid metal structure that absorbs the impact of a train to stop it at the end of the track.

Bullet Trains
The nickname of the high-speed, streamlined passenger trains that operate in Japan.

carriage
An individual compartment of a train that carries the passengers. A carriage is also known as a coach or car.

catenary
An overhead power cable supplying electricity to a train through a pantograph attached to the top of the locomotive.

conductor
The person responsible for the safety of passengers on a train. The conductor checks, and sometimes issues, tickets for passengers on the train.

container
An enormous metal box that transports freight. Containers make it easy to combine different methods of transportation in one journey.

coupling
A connecting device that joins a locomotive to a carriage or wagon to make a train.

coupling rod
A link that connects the driving wheels on both sides of a locomotive. Coupling rods stop the wheels from slipping and even out the power distributed by the steam engine.

cowcatcher
A sloping, V-shaped plate attached to the front of American locomotives. It clears cattle and other obstructions from the line.

cut-and-cover construction
An early method of building underground tunnels. A large trench is cut into the earth along the line of the tunnel, lined with brick and then roofed over. Cut-and-cover construction has been eclipsed by the development of Tunnel-Boring Machines (TBMs).

cylinder
An enclosed part of a steam engine that houses the moving piston.

driving wheel
The wheel of a locomotive that turns in response to power from the cylinder.

flange
A rim on the inside of the metal wheel of a locomotive that stops the wheels slipping sideways and falling off the rails.

freight
Goods transported by rail, road, sea or air.

friction
A force that stops or slows an object moving while it is in contact with another object. Friction results when a train wheel moves over a rail.

funicular
A railway that hauls one car up and one car down steep slopes. Cars move up and down the slope as a cable attached to each carriage winds around an electrically powered drum.

gauge
The width between the inside running edges of the rails of a railway

track. In the USA and most of Europe, the gauge is 1.435m/4ft 8½in.

humpyard
An area beside a main rail route where freight wagons can be sorted to make a freight train. The wagons are pushed over an artificial hill called a hump, and travel by gravity into sidings on the other side.

InterCity Express (ICE)
The name of the high-speed passenger trains that operate in Germany.

leading truck
The pair of leading wheels at the front of a locomotive.

locomotive
An engine powered by steam, diesel or electricity and used to pull the carriages or wagons of a train.

maglev train
A high-speed, streamlined train that is raised above a track called a guideway and moves through the action of powerful electromagnets.

monorail
A train that runs on a single rail.

pantograph
An assembly attached to the top of some locomotives that collects electricity from an overhead power supply. This electricity is then used to move the train.

pendolino
A train that tilts from side to side, enabling the train to move around

curves at higher speeds than non-tilting trains.

piston
A device that moves within the cylinder. Each piston transforms steam pressure into the movement of the wheels of the locomotive.

points
Rails on the track that guide the train's wheels on to a different section of track. Also known as switches.

Pullman
A carriage where passengers can eat or sleep in luxurious surroundings.

rack-and-pinion railway
A railway that operates on steep slopes. A cogwheel underneath the passenger car engages in teeth on a central rail that runs up the slope.

railcar
A self-propelled passenger vehicle powered by diesel or electricity.

rolling stock
The locomotives, carriages, wagons and any other vehicles that operate on a railway.

signals
Messages transmitted to a locomotive to tell the train driver if the track ahead is clear. When the railways first started in the mid-1800s, policemen standing at the side of the track signalled to train drivers with their

hands. Today, electronic signals are transmitted directly to the cabin.

sleeper
1. A horizontal concrete beam, also known as a tie, that supports the rails on a railway track.
2. A carriage that provides sleeping accommodation for passengers.

straddle system
Monorails running on the straddle system rest on a single rail and are balanced and guided by side panels on either side of the train.

train
A number of passenger carriages or freight wagons coupled together. Trains can be self-propelled or hauled by a locomotive.

Train à Grande Vitesse (TGV)
The name of the high-speed, streamlined passenger trains that operate in France.

Train Protection and Warning System (TPWS)
An improved version of the British safety feature AWS. TPWS uses existing AWS safety measures but also incorporates an automatic stop at a red signal and a speed trap in advance of the signal.

Tunnel-Boring Machine (TBM)
A digging device that grinds through soft rock, such as chalk, using a giant, rotating, cutting head.

 # INDEX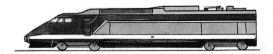